Deferred
Compensation

Deferred Compensation

The New Methodology for Executive Reward

Robert J. Hansman
John W. Larrabee
Hansman McAvoy & Co., Inc.

LexingtonBooks
D.C. Heath and Company
Lexington, Massachusetts
Toronto

Library of Congress Cataloging in Publication Data

Hansman, Robert J.
    Deferred compensation.

    Includes index.
    1. Deferred compensation—Law and legislation—United States.
    2. Deferred compensation—Taxation—Law and legislation—United States.
    3. Executives—Salaries, pensions, etc.—Law and legislation—United States.
    I. Larrabee, John W. II. Title.
    KF1424.H36   1983   344.73'01216   82-48596
    ISBN 0-669-06329-0   347.3041216

Published simultaneously in Canada

Printed in the United States of America

International Standard Book Number: 0-669-06329-0

Library of Congress Catalog Card Number: 82-48596

Contents

Tables

Abbreviations

AICPA	American Institute of Certified Public Accountants
APIIR	Annual Premium Increasing Insurance Rider
ARM	Associate in Risk Management
CIC	Certified Insurance Counselor
CPA	Certified Public Accountant
CPCU	Chartered Property and Casualty Underwriter
CR	Credit
CSO	Commissioners Standard Ordinary
CV	Cash Value
DAR	Defense Acquisition Regulation
DR	Debit
EE	Employee
ER	Employer
ERISA	Employee Retirement Income Security Act of 1974
ERTA	Economic Recovery Tax Act of 1981
FICA	Federal Insurance Contributions Act
FUTA	Federal Unemployment Tax Act
IRA	Individual Retirement Account
IRS	Internal Revenue Service
IRC	Internal Revenue Code
Keough	Self Employed Retirement Plan—House Resolution—10 Keough Act—PL 87-792—1962
LP	Life Paid-up
NPV	Net Present Value
PL	Public Law
RLR	Retired Lives Reserve
TEFRA	Tax Equity and Fiscal Responsibility Act of 1982

Acknowledgments

A list of those professionals and clients who in some way assisted in this book would truly be too long. Many of those generous contributors will find their comments and criticisms have been adapted and have ripened into print. Nevertheless, it would be graceless to omit specific mention of Banker's Life of Iowa, Columbian Mutual Life, New England Life, and Schanker and Puderbach, as well as our associates at Hansman McAvoy & Co., Inc., who freely gave access to certain of their proprietary material. The editing and interpreting of this material is the responsibility of the authors who are culpable for the errors, omissions, and other evils that may have befallen the material.

Introduction

Deferred Compensation, in the past quarter century, has been a part of the financial planning of a substantial number of firms. Fully 95 percent of those firms listed on the New York Stock Exchange are reported as having such plans. A quickening of interest is provoked by the increased democratization of Qualified Plans that is required by the Tax Equity and Act of 1982. The act lowers maximum benefits, discourages top-heavy plans, and obliges employers to vest benefits earlier. One effect is to force some employers to fatten the benefits provided by their existing Qualified Plans with Deferred Compensation in order to complete the benefits promised to senior staffers under the old rules. Another effect is to increase the proportion of plan costs concentrated on the more-transient and lower-paid employees. Thus, to the degree an existing plan has been justified or motivated as a tax-favored device to reward owners, managers, or key employees, the entire rationale now is called into question. This questioning marches across the entire terrain of large and small firms and invites an examination of Deferred Compensation as the alternative. Large size is certainly no impediment but there is a special niche for Deferred Compensation in its application to those smaller, closely held, or totally proprietary firms where its delightful simplicity and exceptional flexibility allow it to resolve differing and changing needs.

This book deals with *Deferred Compensation* as that term is normally understood by practitioners: formalized nonqualified plans in which, however, funding has been arranged. Because of the nature of the tax laws dealing with constructive receipt, that funding would be described by some authorities as informally funded and those with heavier tax orientation as unfunded. This apparent anomaly becomes clear with an understanding of the tax history.

The undergirding principals of Deferred Compensation plans are essentially unchanged since the watershed 1960 IRS Revenue Ruling 60-31. The new ground being broken by this book is in the methodology of designing plans to optimize their inherent advantages and in bringing to those firms considering plans the ingredients for a rational decision. Some part of the need for a new methodology arises from the increased value of money as reflected by interest rates that are quadruple those of one generation ago.

All of the examples are drawn from real-life cases. The identity and a few of the nonsubstantive facts have been altered to provide privacy. This book shares these cases with professional colleagues and others interested in gaining the substantial benefits that Deferred Compensation can provide.

1 The Need for Deferred Compensation

Deferred Compensation can be defined as a contract to pay an employee future benefits for present services. The stream of salary-continuation payments starts upon the death of the employee or his retirement and continues for perhaps fifteen years. In some cases the retirement income is guaranteed for life, and the definite period becomes the minimum payments which the employee or his family will receive should the retired employee die early. The payments thus form a kind of retirement program. It is common to include some special provisions for benefits should the employee become disabled prior to age sixty.

The basic idea is to push funds downstream to a time when they will be needed and, very importantly, when the tax bite for the participants is expected to be lower. In practice, salary-continuation plans are used for two groups of people—the principals of the firm and its key employees. For the principals it is a vehicle with which to arrange their assured retirement and personal financial security and to peel equity from the firm. Its use for key employees is to tie them to the firm with a bond of benefits. For both groups it forms a method of balancing the inequity of the required and optional fringe benefits that are supplied to all the firm's employees. These, by their nature, are disproportionately loaded in favor of the lower paid.

A unique property of these two groups is that they are often relatively close to normal retirement age. It is not surprising that it has taken some time for entrepreneurial success to mature or expertise to develop so that, while funding of retirement can now be contemplated, the funding period is very short. Deferred Compensation plans are uniquely able to address this short-cycle problem.

Discriminatory Advantages of Deferred Compensation

There are, of course, a rather large number of techniques for providing employees with retirement funding, all of which have their place. Indeed, it is not uncommon to use Deferred Compensation as an adjunct to one or another of such plans. The particular niche of Deferred Compensation is a rather broad one because of its great flexibility and the somewhat negative appeal that it is free from the complexity of qualified plans. There are no statutory requirements of minimum coverages or nondiscrimination. In

1

fact, none of that complex body of law and regulation applicable to all other plans applies to Deferred Compensation. It is the essence of Deferred Compensation that it can be totally discriminatory. The employer can select any employee, provide benefits at any age, pick and choose any amount of benefit with essentially no constraints on the maximum and absolutely none required as a minimum. It is the total answer to the complaint that the income-tax structure and mandatory employee-benefit laws give an inadequate consideration for ability and initiative.

Qualified Plans

It is perhaps useful to compare the advantages of Deferred Compensation (or executive salary-continuation plans as they are sometimes called) against those of qualified plans so as to get a good fix on where each type would best fit.

Qualified Plans include all those plans in which the employer is allowed a deduction for the expense of the plan as payments are made into it. The employee is immune from income taxes on the amounts being paid in his behalf and is only taxed upon receipt of the benefits. The several kinds of plans are qualified under different sections of the tax laws. Some are under the profit-sharing section, such as savings and investment plans or Thrift Plans. Some are under the pension section. Some, such as IRAs and Keoughs, have resulted from special legislation. It is useful to make the general distinction between them that they are either defined-contribution plans or defined-benefit plans.

Defined Contribution Plans

Defined-contribution plans are those in which a fixed amount, a formula amount, is paid into the plan each year. An IRA, Keogh, or Thrift Plan would be an example. In such plans the investment success rests with the recipient, and whatever benefit will be generated by the contribution is his reward. These plans are highly discriminatory in favor of lower paid and younger workers and make no allowance for past service before the institution of the plan. As a management tool they are very attractive and useful since they are generally low in cost and highly predictable, being either a flat, per person fee or one tied exactly to earnings with a modest maximum. As a device for compensating the highly motivated and responsible senior staff of the firm, they have little appeal. Consider, for example, a subsidized group IRA's value to a twenty-two-year-old mail-room employee versus a fifty-seven-year-old marketing vice-president. If the contribution is

$2,000 per year for each and the net yield is 12 percent, at age sixty-two the mailroom employee has $1,534,182 and the marketing vice-president has $12,706.

Defined Benefit Plans

Defined-benefit plans and target-benefit plans shift the responsibility for investment success, proper allowances for turnover, mortality, and inflation onto the shoulders of the employer. The employer agrees to provide some definite retirement benefit, such as 50 percent of the final five years of salary. The senior staff of a firm will tend to do better under such plans as benefits are both proportionate to salary and can make allowances for past service prior to establishment of the plan. However, the disadvantages are substantial. Insofar as they are tied to future earnings, the plans tend to be too elastic in price. There have been some real disasters that befell firms and governmental structures with such plans where the promises they made to employees were so swollen by inflation as to far outstrip the funds that had been reserved to meet the obligation.

Rigidity of Qualified Plans

All qualified plans have certain disadvantages in their rigidity. The major restrictions are built around their need to be nondiscriminatory. This includes the obligation to cover all employees (with very minor exceptions), to provide uniform benefits without class or incentive distinctions, and to make some special tests to prevent benefits from being concentrated on the owners and highly paid employees. Imaginative efforts to reward the owners and highly paid with plans which stay within the law, such as Social Security offsets and plans designed to stretch the nondiscrimination rules as far as possible, are only modestly successful in most cases. A temporary advantage is often lost over time since plans extend over many years, and the circumstances that allowed a tricky solution to work may very well change.

Rigidity is not limited to nondiscrimination as such, but extends to rules on the maximum percentage of salary that can be put into the plan as in 401(k) plans, the necessity for involved and often expensive filings for qualification, the necessity to seek IRS consent to stop paying into the plan, the obligation to support other pension plans that have failed, and a host of tedious periodic filings for ERISA and the IRS.

The Tax Deductibility Issue

The apparent advantage of qualified plans hangs by the tax treatment. It is an article of faith in tax planning to get the money off the tax rolls for as long as possible and to make every expense a tax-deductible item. Company-wide benefit plans using the qualified approach often fit nicely into this formula. For those whom Deferred Compensation is to aid, the benefits are likely to be ephemeral or worse.

Since the accumulation of funds for Deferred Compensation is internal, that is, they are owned by the company and not transferred out, there is little or no cost to be expensed during the accumulation period. Therefore, the fact that any expenses are not deductible may be unimportant. The fact that the benefits that are paid after the retirement or death of the employee are deductible allows the employer a stream of future deductions, as well as the discounted net present value of the funds that have been developed to meet the obligation. Said another way, the employer can fund a very attractive package of future benefits at a low cost that recognizes those benefits will be tax-deductible business deductions and will be discountable because they are to be paid over time.

It is not hard to find corporate taxpayers whose tax rate is substantially lower than that of its principals and key employees. Tax-loss carry forwards, accelerated cost recovery through the new depreciation rules, and simply lower corporate tax rates of the Economic Recovery Tax Act of 1981 all may mean that the current deductibility of payments to a qualified plan have very little value. In fact, it may be better for owners to allow the accumulation of Deferred Compensation funding within a corporation controlled by them. For example, take a medical doctor or attorney operating as a professional corporation whose personal tax rate is 50 percent. If, rather than stripping out all the earnings, some were left in, say $25,000, the lower corporate tax rate (15 percent starting in 1983) would mean $21,500 could be being accumulated rather than the $12,500 if taken out as salary. The existence of a Deferred Compensation agreement eliminates the danger that the firm would be held responsible for an excess accumulation of profits and exposed to that penalty tax. Although the new law raised the limit to $250,000 for some firms, the limit for professional corporations and some other services organizations continues at $150,000.

Reversing Reverse Discrimination

Again, the most important ingredient in a Deferred Compensation plan is the fact that it is discriminatory. Even the most superficial examination of a well-designed plan will often reveal that the ability to accomplish the intended result without carrying excess baggage will more than offset the greatest tax leverage developed in a plan that does not have that flexibility. When the cost of fringe benefits provided to employees is measured as a percentage of salary to obtain an effort index, it will become obvious how slanted to lower-paid employees is the total package: state unemployment, federal unemployment, FICA, group medical, disability income, dental insurance, vacation, cafeterias, qualified profit sharing, pension plans, and others are all either flat priced or have caps that, at least partially, disenfranchise senior staff.

Social Security Slanted to Low Incomes

It may be excessively pessimistic to predict that the Social Security system will collapse and that no benefits will be paid to those who retire in future years. On the other hand, one can be less sanguine about how well those with high average earnings will be treated. The payments are already curved to favor those with low average earnings. A further move in that direction is being undertaken, and it seems reasonable to predict that political considerations will reduce benefits to a simple floor for the lowly paid. The Deferred Compensation plan is an ideal method to make a partial redressing of these imbalances.

Security for the Firm

Deferred Compensation plans are usually focused on the owners and managers of the firm. For this reason the parameters of what is important to the participants may be in dramatic contrast to a plan that addresses the retirement needs of all employees. Those who are not either owners or managers may have only a mild interest in the survival and success of the firm, particularly if they have highly transferable skills. This understandable disinterest is magnified in the matter of retirement benefits. Such an employee would quite rightly prefer that any funding of his retirement benefits be strictly divorced from the success or survival of the firm. Insured qualified plans ideally answer this need. All of the funds are irrevocably transferred beyond any control of the employer so whatever disaster befalls the firm will in no way endanger whatever funding has been made for the employee. Additional safeguards for insolvent pension plans and distribution rules for terminated pension plans are part of the current laws that provide increasing security for the employee.

An entirely different pattern of motivation applies to the typical participant of a Deferred Compensation plan. As owners or managers they have a vital concern with the present survival and success of the company. It would not be atypical to find that they have no real opportunity to obtain employment at anywhere near the earnings they can gain from the firm or to obtain any employment at all. They may also have essentially all, or at least the core of their wealth, tied up in the firm so that threats to its survival may threaten ruin. For these reasons the prospective retiree of the Deferred Compensation class has quite the opposite view of the irrevocable transfer out of significant sums of money from which the firm is absolutely foreclosed access. Financial planners working in the area of Retired Life Reserve will recognize the resistance they experience, even in the face of highly beneficial results, when that entails the absolute loss of control of a large amount of money.

Aside from the negative aspect of the loss of control of capital and its potential for endangering the survival of the firm, Deferred Compensation plans buttress the positive side of the firm's present and its future. The existence of an important asset, earmarked though it is for a particular and very important purpose, creates opportunity. The sudden opportunity to buy out a competitor, a dramatic need for more working capital to meet a huge order, ballast on the balance sheet for borrowing strength, funds to meet an attractive offer to redeem shares of the corporate stock, and surely many other needs can be imagined in which extra cash could tip the balance and provide the owners and managers with a large profit or increase in worth. Not the least of possible needs might be that of nourishing nepotism. Deferred Compensation participants are often those whose objectives may be primarily, or almost exclusively, the perpetuation of the firm as a family resource and activity. The survival of the firm in the hands of children or relatives may assure a secure retirement beyond what the Deferred Compensation plan would provide.

Internalizing the funds being accumulated for the safety net, and those that drop to the bottom line as surplus from a death, can add considerable strength to the objectives of the owners and managers. The highest and best application of Deferred Compensation for reasons of tax and funds flow is obtained when the firm survives and prospers. The offsetting vulnerability of the funds to the errors of mismanagement and claims that other creditors may have against the firm is not to be ignored. For the kinds of people usually included as participants in Deferred Compensation, the hazard is overbalanced by the increased security that flexibility associated with control of the funds affords.

Every firm's overall disaster plan should include a strategy to make a timely reversal in the Deferred Compensation plan, extract proceeds, and capture for the owners and managers as much of the benefits as can be arranged. The fact that the participants are also the insiders makes such a strategy practical and possible to implement. This remote contingency represents nothing worse to most of the participants than the collapse of the firm due to the absence of capital that was irrevocably transferred out and unavailable to buttress another dark day.

The right to hold any funds in the name of the firm and off the tax rolls is limited by a tax-hungry IRS. The IRS view is that reserves for unidentified contingencies are designed to avoid tax on the dividends that would be distributed if there were no reserve. Under the 1981 Economic Recovery Act the amount that could be reserved—over and above the amount needed to meet the reasonable needs of the business—without special penalty taxation was raised from $150,000 to $250,000 (except in the case of service organizations where it remains at $150,000). The Deferred Compensation plan, because it constitutes a definite measurable future obligation, thwarts this limitation. There is no limit to the amount that may be accumulated to meet the future obligations of the firm under a Deferred Compensation plan other than that those future obligations for income to employees not constitute of themselves unreasonable or excessive compensation to the individual employees.

2

A Flaw in the Traditional Approach

Need for a Change

A great deal of life insurance has been purchased in the past quarter century to fund Deferred Compensation plans, much to the benefit of the participants and, presumably, also to the companies and their representatives who underwrote those plans. The changing pattern of investment yield calls into question the methodology used for funding these plans or at the very least the manner in which professionals design them. A redesign is needed to salvage the underlying concept and to avoid a contest on prospective-investment yield that is of doubtful advantage to the insurer and clearly to the detriment of the plan participants.

The Traditional Approach

Table 2-1 is taken from a highly respected and authoritative text, *Deferred Compensation,* edited by Herbert Chasman and published by Dow-Jones Irwin in 1978. The explanation of this traditional approach takes the following course: the first segment shows the effect of funding with life insurance on the surplus position of the firm during the lifetime of the employee. Attention is drawn to the crossover point where the gain in surplus exceeds the total premiums paid (at age sixty) and to the greater gain and sufficiency of cash to fund the benefit at age sixty-five.

The second segment, columns four, five, and six, shows the proceeds upon the death of the insured. Here one sees the excess of insurance proceeds over the premiums paid, for example, at age sixty where the firm would have a gain of $57,995 over the total premiums paid. The third segment points up the tax deductibility of payments to the employee.

The explanation goes on to point out that the key columns are six, nine, and ten because they represent the two tax forces at work. The first shows that the proceeds flow into the firm's surplus free of income tax. The second shows that the proceeds that are paid out to the employee are tax deductible and thus the firm enjoys a gain as indicated in column ten.

Some Flaws Are Obvious

Redesigning the plan to one funded with mortality uses all the same elements but positions the firm to optimize the tax advantages and improve

9

Table 2-1
Deferred Compensation (Salary Continuation) Plan Informally Funded with Life Insurance

Annual premium: $4,407
Male, current age forty-five
Special executive Deferred Compensation
Benefits to be provided by employer
Death benefit: $100,000 if death occurs prior to retirement
Retirement benefit: $10,000 per year for ten years starting at age sixty-five
Face amount: $100,000
Plan: paid up at age sixty-five
Dividends used to purchase paid-up additions

	Results While Executive Lives					Results When Executive Dies				
1	*2*	*3*		*4*	*5*	*6*	*7*	*8*	*9*	*10*
Total premiums to date	Asset value of policy (cash value)[a+b]	Reduction (−) or gain (+) in surplus	Insured's Attained age	Total death benefit during prior year of age[a]	Total premiums to date	Excess of death benefit over premiums paid	Death benefit payments: to heirs	Tax credit on payments	After-tax cost of payments	Gain/loss to surplus (columns 6-9)
$ 4,407	$ 2,072	$ −2,335	46	$100,000	$ 4,407	$95,593	$100,000	$50,000	$50,000	$45,593
22,035	16,862	−5,173	50	102,647	22,035	80,612	100,000	50,000	50,000	30,612
44,070	40,467	−3,603	55	110,804	44,070	66,734	100,000	50,000	50,000	16,734
66,105	71,204	+5,099	60	124,100	66,105	57,995	100,000	50,000	50,000	7,995
88,140	111,147	+23,077	65	141,552	88,140	53,412	100,000	50,000	50,000	3,412
88,140	134,487	+46,347	70	161,704	88,140	73,564	100,000	50,000	50,000	23,564
88,140	161,367	+73,227	75	184,526	88,140	96,386	100,000	50,000	50,000	46,386

Source: Herbert Chasman, *Deferred Compensation* (Homewood, Ill.: Dow Jones-Irwin, 1978). Reprinted with permission.
Note: Assuming 50 percent tax bracket for corporation.
[a]Dividends are based on current scale. They are neither guarantees nor estimates, future dividends will depend on experience.
[b]Guaranteed cash value plus cash value of dividend additions.

its results or those of the participant. Simple inspection of the traditional presentation in table 2-1, without any higher mathematics, suggests that the plan is most profitable or most beneficial when mortality is brought into play and weakest when it is inspected as a vehicle with which to accumulate funds with which to retire at age sixty-five. A properly designed mortality-funded plan is *not* a vehicle with which to accumulate funds at age sixty-five! Look again at segment number one. By mortality-funding standards it gets the design of the plan off on the wrong foot. Almost involuntarily attention is drawn to what appears to be a rather bad investment. By *investing* $4,407 per year for twenty years, one winds up with $111,147 or 2.37 percent interest on the money. To look at it another way, how many employees would forgo a salary increase of $4,407 for twenty years to get a ten-year income of $10,000 per year? Even the simplest of souls has some intuitive grasp of the time value of money and, given current interest rates, would approach that decision cautiously. The plain fact is that the really valid use of any cash value generated by a Deferred Compensation plan is only as a necessary corollary of getting the mortality portion of the plan paid up during the working life of the employee and incidentally (but not insignificantly) as a safety net.

Finding the Strength of a Well-Designed Plan

If the best use of the tax leverage on which such plans are hung depends upon mortality, it obviously makes sense to load the plan as heavily as possible in that direction. In this traditional example the mortality portion of $100,000 is overbalanced by the equity portion or the building of cash values. There is little inducement for the employer to make much of an effort to gain the small advantage involved, and this will always be so when there is a small gap between the policy equity and the face value. Apart from the disadvantage to the plan participants, it would seem that the life-insurance industry would perceive that its strength is not in head-to-head conflict with other investment media, but in its mastery of mortality and the excellent tax leverage that it affords.

Overfunding Weakens the Benefits

Even the inexpert buyer will wonder why the plan in table 2-1 has been designed to generate $111,147 in order to fund payments of $10,000 for ten years starting at age sixty-five. If money will earn 9 percent at that time it only requires $64,176. If 14 percent is available, $52,161 will do it. If, in addition, one believes that the firm or its successor will be in the 50 percent tax bracket and enjoy the deductibility of the payments, one needs only half of that, or $26,080.

A More-Meaningful Stream of Payments

Since Deferred Compensation is designed for participants and in most cases the participants are also the decision makers, it makes good sense to optimize the benefits giving them the advantage of the tax leverage and the best array of benefits. A flow of funds of $10,000 per year starting at age sixty-five would not be unwelcome, but age seventy-five seems to be a bad place to run out of money. Age eighty would be a good bit more attractive, and an endless stream for a lifetime would be even better than that. Of course, it would cost more. The net present value jumps from $26,080 on the assumptions made to $30,710; this would cover fifteen years rather than ten years. One may think of that as a 50 percent increase in benefit, but it only required 18 percent more funding.

A Lifetime Income Can Be Provided

Interestingly enough that same amount could provide the funds for life. The life expectancy of the forty-five-year-old employee will not get him to age eighty, and even if he reaches age sixty-five the probability that he'll live much beyond eighty is small. The cautious employer will probably enjoy the comfort of seeing an annuity priced for various ages to capture the concept that a guaranteed stream of fifteen payments starting at age sixty-five could be more expensive than the same size payments for life, but with a somewhat smaller guarantee of minimum payments, such as ten years or less.

Assumptions for a Redesigned Plan

Funding Deferred Compensation involves making some assumptions. The employer should be comfortable with the assumptions, and they should be periodically reviewed to see that they are holding. If one uses somewhat more modern assumptions, one can redesign the traditional approach to a more attractive package of benefits in which the full thrust of tax forces and current interest rates are enjoyed. Assume the same male, age forty-five with $4,400 available to initiate the plan, a tax rate of the employer at 46 percent, and that funds being held by the firm and invested in its operations or elsewhere will yield 16 percent.

A Brighter Batch of Benefits

Table 2-2 shows a rather remarkable increase in benefits using the same amount of funding. The income has jumped from $10,000 per year to

Table 2-2
Deferred Compensation Using Mortality Funding
Annual premium: $4,393
Male, current age forty-five
Benefit: $20,000 per year for fifteen years starting at death or age sixty-five (guaranteed lifetime retirement with lesser certain period is an option)
Policy: $195,000 life with premiums to age ninety-five using dividend to buy paid-up additions

Remaining Value @ $20,000 Year	Employer Obligation Benefits to EE or Family NPV[a] @ 16 Percent	Tax Credit @ 46 Percent	Net Cost to Employer	Age	Funds Available Ultimately (at death)	Safety Net If No Death[b]	Expected Value[c]	Surplus Activity Disbursed Cumulative Premium	Net Reduction or Gain
$300,000	$111,509	$51,292	$60,217	46	$195,513	—	—	$ 4,393	$ (4,216)
300,000	111,509	51,292	60,217	50	201,722	—	—	21,965	(3,928)
300,000	111,509	51,292	60,217	55	215,171	—	—	43,930	2,645
300,000	111,509	51,292	60,217	60	236,409	—	—	65,895	1,732
300,000	111,509	51,292	60,217	65	267,418	$124,056	$159,609	87,900	36,156
200,000	96,665	44,465	52,200	70	309,139	185,883	232,970	114,218	76,665
100,000	65,485	30,123	35,302	75	358,032	246,458	307,382	136,183	110,275
None	None	None	None	80	412,356	314,566	384,099	158,148	156,418

[a] Net present value.

[b] Cash value available to fund living benefits if firm can not meet obligation from current earnings.

[c] Expected value: this important concept in the funding-with-mortality decision process is treated in subsequent chapters.

$20,000 per year. The minimum guaranteed period of benefits has jumped from ten years to fifteen. Although it is simplistic to look at it that way, the total benefit package has jumped from $100,000 to $300,000. In addition, the option of a lifetime income of $20,000 per year starting at age sixty-five is offered in lieu of the fifteen year plan. This plan makes it much more attractive for the employee to forgo a currently taxable $4,400 salary increase, particularly if he foresees a lower tax rate for himself when he reaches age sixty-five. The plan *still* returns a profit to the firm if the assumptions on which he agreed prove to have been correct. Table 2-2 also shows the safety net in action.

But Is It Safe?

Projecting any financial program into the future is necessarily limited in its accuracy. The ability of the firm to make future premium payments, the nature of the future tax laws, the return on investments, and a host of other factors could alter the results. Every major long-term financial plan obviously needs careful periodic reviews. The question here is how safe is safe? This plan still works if the firm gets *no* tax credit for payments it makes to the employee (or his beneficiary) and if it can earn 13.8 percent on its investments. This plan still works *no matter when* death occurs even if the firm gets no tax deduction for payments to the employee's beneficiary if it can earn anything over 5.9 percent on its investment. Also, after the first year, the firm would turn a substantial profit. Safety is subjective. If the employer is insufficiently comforted by the safety net, the assumptions can be made more conservative and the plan designed to fit them. If change is required in an ongoing plan, it can usually be accomplished easily. Since most changes are only evolutionary, not revolutionary, they seldom produce drastic changes in the periodic funding.

Funding Media

Any number of life-insurance contracts could be used to meet the assumptions. The maximum tax leverage is gained when the gap between the death benefit and the policy cash values is greatest, but that gap is limited by the assumptions. The gap also vitiates the arguments of those who would seek to compete with life insurance by treating it as simply an investment and ignoring the importance of the mortality portion. Life with premiums to age ninety-five, as used here, provides some extra flexibility. The usual axiom in Deferred Compensation is that the funding of the plan should be in place during the working life of the employee. Whole life with premiums to age ninety-five (LP-95), with the dividends used to buy additions, will meet that test. The firm could discontinue premium payments at the employee's age sixty-five and have a sufficiently large paid-up policy to meet its obligations. On the other hand, the cash value of the policy is increasing at about double the amount of the annual premium. If cash requirements do not make adding to surplus uncomfortable, this may be the option to elect. The health of the employee also enters into the election. If he were in doubtful health, the option to continue premium payments and adversely select against the insurance company should be elected. The cash to fund future premium payments could be borrowed from the policy equity at 8 percent interest. This interest would be a tax-deductible expense for the firm. The stop-start features implicit in this kind of funding have been treated in chapter 11.

Table 2-3 shows continuation of the premium payments to age eighty with no death. At that point the firm's obligation would have ended. It

Table 2-3
Impact on Surplus If No Death Occurs before Age Eighty
Assumptions:
Tax and interest assumptions are unchanged
Employer continues to pay $4,393 on policy after age sixty-five
Retirement payments are deducted from surplus net of tax
($20,000 − $9,200 = $10,800) and paid for fifteen years

			Surplus			
			Net		Remaining	
		Reductionary	Reduction	Increasing	Balance	Face
	Beginning	Premium	by Paying	Cash	at Year	Amount
Age	Balance	Payment	Employee	Value	End	of Policy
64					$124,056	$259,940
65	$124,056	($4,393)	($10,800)	$ 9,377	118,240	267,416
66	118,240	(4,393)	(10,800)	9,920	112,967	275,132
67	112,967	(4,393)	(10,800)	10,099	107,873	283,126
68	107,873	(4,393)	(10,800)	10,499	103,179	291,430
69	103,179	(4,393)	(10,800)	10,740	98,726	300,097
70	98,726	(4,393)	(10,800)	11,192	94,725	309,139
71	94,725	(4,393)	(10,800)	11,404	90,936	318,477
72	90,936	(4,393)	(10,800)	11,789	87,532	328,061
73	87,532	(4,393)	(10,800)	12,162	84,501	337,863
74	84,501	(4,393)	(10,800)	12,334	81,642	347,859
75	81,642	(4,393)	(10,800)	12,886	79,335	358,032
76	79,335	(4,393)	(10,800)	13,048	77,190	368,389
77	77,190	(4,393)	(10,800)	13,225	75,222	378,389
78	75,222	(4,393)	(10,800)	13,798	73,827	389,783
79	73,827	(4,393)	(10,800)	13,805	72,439	400,899
80	72,439	(4,393)	—	14,232	82,279	412,356
			($162,000)			

[a]One insurance company specializing in annuities offers a $10,800 immediate annuity ($900 per month) for life with ten years certain for $86,000—male sixty-five. Although it would seldom be the best course under present tax rules, the $124,056 cash value could be used to buy an annuity and have $38,056 remaining.

would have excess surplus of $82,279 or a tax-free mortality infusion for a death in that year of $412,356. Since the insurance-policy cash values have already been bookkept as surplus, and that surplus reduced by the payments to the employee, the addition to surplus is only $168,059. The surplus, which is now cash, stands at $250,356. There are myriad ways in which the firm could handle the plan when the employee reaches sixty-five, and thereafter what will be best can only be determined at that time. The important point is that the options remain open.

3 Probability and Its Application

Probability and statistics are essential tools in sophisticated managerial decisions. When a variety of solutions are possible, the ability to assign a probability to each allows a decision based on the most likely outcome. In any one result the decision may not prove to have been the most advantageous, but in the long run, if the probabilities were correctly assigned, the best overall decisions will have been made.

Probabilities are drawn from three sources. First, some situations have their probabilities inherent in them. For example, the probability of picking the king of hearts from a deck of cards at random will be one in fifty-two; or the chance of getting a three on one throw of a die will be one in six. Second, intuitive probabilities are a kind of educated guess drawn from experience and logic. They are not as accurate of course as the selection of the king of hearts but are by no means useless in making business decisions. The third type of probability is drawn from historical experience. It can be highly reliable as a device for forecasting the future if (a) the number of samples was sufficiently large to form an accurate picture of the past and (b) there have been no significant changes in the circumstances under which the data was accumulated.

In the case of mortality dealt with here, both of the factors necessary for a good future forecast are in place. The Commissioner's Standard Ordinary (CSO) Table of Mortality, 1958, when properly used, will predict with a high degree of reliability the probability of the death of an individual in any given period of time. Another basic concept of probability enters into the calculation to be performed. That is the formula for determining the probability that at least one of a series of unrelated events will occur. It is simply the sum of the individual probabilities. The probability of mortality within a group is the sum of the individual mortality probabilities. The perceptive reader will recognize that other possibilities exist such as the probability that more than one death might occur. These are sufficiently remote (although they can of course be calculated) as to be safely ignored.

To find the probability of mortality for an individual prior to age sixty-five refer to the 1958 CSO Table of Mortality (see appendix A). First, find the number of people living at a specific, selected age. Second, look up the number living at age sixty-five. Subtracting this number from the first one will give the number of deaths prior to age sixty-five. Finally, dividing the number of deaths by the first number will give the probability of mortality

Table 3-1

Male, Age Forty-Five, Has Probability of Death prior to Age Sixty-Five of 24.85 Percent

Step 1. Number living at age 45	9,048,999
Step 2. Number living at age 65	6,800,531
Step 3. Number of deaths (step 1 minus step 2)	2,248,468
Step 4. Probability of mortality (2,248,468 ÷ 9,048,999)	0.24847

Based on 1958 CSO Table of Mortality.

for an individual prior to a selected age (see table 3-1). Utilizing this same mathematical process one can easily determine the probability of death for any individual in a group prior to a specific age or within a specific time span. Note that as the formula for determining the probability that at least one of a series of unrelated events will occur is the sum of the individual probabilities, so the probability of a death occurring within a group is the sum of the individual probabilities.

Table 3-2 shows that there is a 53 percent chance of a death occurring in the sample group (three lives) in a twenty-year period. In other words, there is a possibility of three deaths and a probability of .5264 deaths. This concept becomes important in funding with mortality since the firm will have considerably more money to meet its obligations if a death occurs than if no death occurs. To plan on no deaths artificially exaggerates the need for nondeath funds.

Table 3-2

Probability of Death before Oldest Participant Reaches Age Sixty-Five (Twenty Years)

Age	Number Living[a]	Age	Number Living	Probability of Death
45	9,048,999	65	6,800,531	.2484
40	9,241,359	60	7,698,698	.1669
35	9,373,807	55	8,331,317	.1112
Probability of death				0.5265

[a]Based on 1958 CSO Table of Mortality.

4

Funding Deferred Compensation with Mortality

The Tax Leverage of Mortality

The underlying concept of funding Deferred Compensation with mortality relies on the tax-free flow of funds provided by life insurance. The well-established tax situation is that the proceeds of a life-insurance policy paid at death are received by the firm without being taxed either as income or capital gains. The logic is that inasmuch as the premiums were not deductible, the tax on the policy has been paid even if it ripens into a huge sum after the payment of as little as one premium. Some measure of the significance of this can be perceived by imagining the death in the first policy year of a male insured for $500,000 whose firm paid a $4,000 premium. The $500,000 goes directly to the firm's surplus without being taxed. If the firm is in the 46 percent tax bracket it would take earnings of $925,926 to have a similar affect. Assuming further that the firm makes a 10 percent profit on its sales, the result is equivalent to additional sales in that period of $9,259,259.

After selecting a policy amount that will provide all of the funds needed to provide the employee or his family with the promised benefits, the employer arranges to have the policy paid up during the productive period of the employee's work life and before his retirement. Although the premium payments are not tax deductible, and clearly this is preferable to having the proceeds taxable, they are largely balanced by the growing cash values to which the employer keeps title. After a few years the cash values exceed the premiums paid, but this gain is also free of taxation as long as the employer does not take the gain. The impact on surplus essentially becomes a rearrangement: cash is taken from surplus to pay the premium and the cash values are added back to surplus as a highly liquid asset which can be reduced to cash or borrowed against at a predetermined low rate of interest (the interest is a deductible business expense).

The Safety Net

Although this buildup of cash or loan values on the balance sheet of the employer is not the prime funding source for the Deferred Compensation plan (that function is handled by the life-insurance policy proceeds), it does form a contingency reserve. Normal funding of the period payments to participants

19

would be supplied either by the proceeds of the life-insurance policy if a death had occurred or from the current earnings of the firm. The contingency reserve simply acts as a safety net should the firm have insufficient cash available. Typically, at age sixty-five the reserve would be from 30 percent to 60 percent of the face value of the life-insurance policy and can be varied as needed. Of course the plan cost would be proportionately altered as well. Where several employees are included in a Deferred Compensation plan the cumulative probability of a death and the resulting tax-free flow of funds can be assessed. This avoids the temptation to overfund the contingency reserve (see table 4-1).

Disability

The opportunity exists in most Deferred Compensation plans to obtain a premium waiver provision that will assure the funding will continue without payments by the firm should a participant become disabled prior to age sixty. As the disability may be prolonged before death or recovery, and the productivity of the employee lost, it is usually wise to buy this low-cost funding insurance. In some plans the disabled employee is given the amount of net after-tax payment that is waived on the theory that the firm's commitment to a specific level of funding allows this without any increase in cost to the employer. Most authorities feel this is a separate issue which should be handled with disability income protection, group long-term disability, or a combination of the two.

Provisional Participants

The discriminatory advantage of Deferred Compensation allows it to be used to capture new key employees or reach down to junior ranks and single out participants whose loyalty the firm desires to guarantee. However, the firm may wish to defer fully funding the plan for reasons of cash flow, the uncertainty of continued employment, or other factors. This objective is easily

Table 4-1
Probability of Death

Age	Number Living[a]	Age	Number Living	Probability of Death
45	9,048,999	65	6,800,531	.2484
40	9,241,359	60	7,698,698	.1669
40	9,373,807	55	8,331,317	.1112
Probability of death				0.5265

[a]Based on 1958 CSO Table of Mortality.

handled by a low-cost, term-insurance policy which bridges the period until full funding is undertaken but which completes the premature death obligation. The aggregate probability of mortality is, of course, increased, which increases the stability of the plan. Death of a specific employee creates a large infusion of cash and a stretched out, long-term cash obligation. Thus a favorable funds flow is produced which can be a buffer for the loss of a key person.

More Leverage from Taxes and Funds Flow

In addition to the tax leverage of having the proceeds of the life-insurance policy drop directly to the bottom line, the mortality-funded Deferred Compensation plan takes further advantage of the continued existence of the firm beyond the death or retirement of the participant. The payments that are made by the firm after a death or retirement are deductible expenses to the firm. Consequently, they will be paid with fifty-four-cent dollars or seventy-cent dollars or whatever dollars reflect the current tax rate of the firm.

Where the funds are in place at the beginning of the obligation to the employee or his estate, it is obviously appropriate to discount the stream of net-after-tax payments with a rate of interest appropriate to the firm. This could be the rate at which the firm borrows money, the rate at which it could invest the money, or perhaps the rate of return that it enjoys on its invested capital. The bulge of money that comes from a death, significantly enough, comes at the time of losing a key employee. The buttressing of the firm's financial statement from inflow and the increased liquidity with which to patch over the loss of a key employee is an important adjunct.

Survival of the Firm

Since the highest and best use of the mortality-funded Deferred Compensation plan arises out of the continuation of the firm, the safety net assists in assuring that continuation. The exact format of the firm's continuation may not be too important—partnership, corporation, successor firm, merged firm, and so on—because the funding and the obligation can be arranged to follow that thread. Conceivably the obligation to provide future compensation to certain people and the assets with which to meet these obligations, together with the tax advantages on both sides of that equation, could be the only assets or liabilities remaining in the firm; this would still be an attractive package for its continuation or assumption by a successor. Building the safety net to the right level assures this.

Quantifying the Safety Net

The measurement of the safety net can be developed mathematically using some technique for the calculation of the net present value of a cash flow such as

$$PV = PMT \; \frac{1 - (1 + i)^{-N}}{i}$$

and that for making investment decisions under uncertainty where probability for the various possibilities can be assigned.

$$E(R) = \sum_{i=1}^{n} R_i P_i$$

Using these two formulae the probable posture of the safety net can be accurately determined at any given point in time. The assumptions can be varied so that any combination of tax and interest effects can be seen. This allows funding to a level appropriate to the type of firm, its circumstances, and the comfort level desired by the principals—neither too high nor too low.

A further worst-case analysis can be made that measures not the *probable* posture of the safety net but posture without the assumption of any mortality. At any given point that possibility does, of course, exist. Again, various assumptions as to interest and taxes can be cranked into the calculation. When there is more than one participant, the aggregate probability of mortality following the predicted path increases following the law of large numbers. The safety net is also reinforced by the sum of the funds being generated for each participant. The collective funds can be compared with the emerging liability as each participant reaches the age to begin receiving retirement benefits. (It should be noted here that throughout this text the payments, premiums, fund flows, and other factors are treated as annual amount to avoid unnecessarily complicating the concepts. The reader will recognize that benefits are more often paid monthly, a fact which would alter the amounts somewhat. It will also be evident that in some instances the use of "annuity due" rather than an "annuity" would have been more accurate. Hopefully, the benefits of simplicity outweigh the inaccuracies.)

Need to Review

It is axiomatic that, in dealing with probabilities, nothing can be 100 percent certain or, in fact, one is not dealing with probabilities at all. The purpose here is to attempt to quantify the data to a point where a rational managerial decision can be made. It is important that the cost of a Deferred Compensation plan be at the lowest possible level consistent with the level of certainty the participants require. Risk-transfer decisions are inherently subjective, and the best ones are made with the best information. As with any such project, a periodic review (at least annually) should be made to test that the plan is on track and that assumptions are holding.

5 A Bond of Benefits

Capturing and Keeping Key Employees

In many cases the prime reason for installing a Deferred Compensation plan is to help retain or attract employees with skills essential to the success of the firm. Often this objective is met by holding the person for a relatively short period such as six or seven years. By that time the employee can be expected to have settled in, become old enough to be less likely to be making career jumps, and the firm may have established its own level of success so that it can no longer be outbid for these skills, or it has more ready access to alternatives. An example might be a conscientious controller in his middle forties who, because the firm is still in transition to profitability, is somewhat underpaid. If he can be retained until reaching his early fifties, the probability of his leaving is greatly reduced, and presumably by that time the firm could go into the marketplace and find and afford an adequate replacement. The problem is to retain this employee without disrupting the expense side of the ledger. Confronted with this problem or the need to attract an outsider with very special skills, it may behoove the employer to consider the installation of a low-cost Deferred Compensation plan which, by any definition, would be considered generous. Because the costs of these generous future benefits can be funded gradually, and indeed be discounted to their present value, the impact on the firm's earnings statement can be minimal but very significant to the individual.

Customized Vesting Schedules

One key for tying the employee to the firm with a bond of benefits, or golden handcuffs, is the vesting schedule. The term *vesting* in Deferred Compensation has a somewhat different meaning than it does in qualified pension or profit-sharing plans. There it means the unqualified title and all ownership rights to the benefit. In Deferred Compensation it is taken to mean only the successful completion of two of the major hurdles—that of service with the firm and of reaching a certain age. However, the benefit often remains subject to forfeit for breach of the covenant not to compete. The IRS has determined in Revenue Ruling 71-419 that there is no constructive receipt if the Deferred Compensation agreement is entered into before the compensation is earned and the employer's promise to pay is not secured in any way. The noncompete provision is not a tax essential but may be an important business adjunct.

Just as the Deferred Compensation plan is not bound by the constraints of nondiscrimination, so it is not restricted by rigid vesting as demanded by ERISA-governed and IRS-qualified plans. This becomes a particular advantage when the very top layers of a firm are being provided with substantial funding for their retirement. More than one firm has unintentionally created a rival and drained away talent critical to its own success by allowing for the creation of sufficient capital in the hands of senior staffers with entrepreneurial ambitions of their own. Not only does the different definition of vesting in Deferred Compensation, with its unending noncompete and consulting obligations, defeat this, but the vesting itself can be delayed until a time when there would be no threat of a spinning off of the participants into a new competitor.

It is often better to gain the enthusiasm of the participants by allowing an easy vesting because the noncompete will prevent competition, and the benefit is more real to the employee when he sees that it can be easily achieved. The usual method of balancing easy vesting, where the employee has satisfied the age and service requirement before the normal retirement date, is to reduce the benefits proportionately if the employee does not persist in his employment until the normal retirement date. The funding of the plan thus tracks with the years of productive employment of the employee. It is also usual to defer any benefits for retirement until the normal retirement date. Consequently, an employee who is vested at age fifty-five might leave the firm but still get some retirement payments starting at age sixty-five. As with all elements of Deferred Compensation, the rules are very elastic. Where the participants are the principals, it may be desired to forego many of these restrictions more suited to high-level support people.

Vesting and Funding Targets

It is usual to make no service or age requirement for the stream of benefits that begin at the death of a participant, although no barrier exists to doing that. It is also not uncommon to have no vesting schedule, particularly when dealing with principals. The vesting is most often used to assure employees that they will not be denied the benefits they have earned by some caprice on the part of the employer. As such, it is sometimes useful to design a schedule that can be applied impartially to all participants but gives the desired results. Innumerable possibilities exist such as years of service, a certain age, or some weighted mix of the two. One easy method uses the simple sum of the age and service to reach a given number such as seventy. That would mean a fifty-five-year-old employee with fifteen years of service would be vested or a sixty-year-old with ten years of service. This type of formula is useful where the participants include the principals, and they wish to vindicate early vesting on their behalf, because most often the principals have the longest service.

Funding targets may be applicable when the plan extends downward to second-echelon employees at relatively young ages. For reasons of current cash flow and in anticipation of some turnover, the firm may elect to limit the funding for such employees to the death-only benefit and omit the safety net until a certain age or service level (or combination) is reached. Depending upon how much or little the employer wishes to disclose, this can be a threshold which denotes an additional level of acceptance of the junior employee or only a financial-planning target by the firm. Some agreements with participants speak to the issue of how the funding will be handled, and of course good accounting and managerial practice requires that the safety net should be accrued in a systematic and rational manner over the period of active employment. However, it is self-evident that future services which the employer expects to receive from a young employee can be commensurate with a modest deferral of full funding.

6 A Sample Case: Testing Inc.

Testing Inc. was founded twenty years ago by the Colby brothers, Tom and Bill, and Tom's classmate George Ryan. Five years ago the Colby's brother-in-law, Ken Williams, joined the firm as its treasurer. These four principals own over 90 percent of the stock in the company. They deliberately kept their salaries low to ensure their firm's success, and indeed, the company has flourished. Today it has sales of $3,000,000 and employs over forty people.

The majority of Testing Inc.'s employees are highly paid technical people, many with doctorates in the sciences. A half dozen have been with the company almost since its founding. A generous package of fringe benefits is provided, and a recent study by Williams showed that the average employee costs the firm 39 percent in addition to salary. This included medical insurance, life insurance, income insurance, workers-compensation insurance, FICA, unemployment, thrift plan, group IRA, and dental insurance. In contrast, the percentage for the top four executives is only 21 percent.

To address this imbalance, and to provide retirement and family security for the executives, Williams has undertaken an investigation of various retirement plans. Certain contracts with the Department of Defense, which is the largest single customer for Testing Inc., permit Williams to plan on an annual expenditure of about $50,000 per year for the next five years. Given this information, census data on all the employees, and the objective of weighting the plans as heavily as possible for the four principals, Testing Inc.'s brokers solicited plan designs from various insurance company providers. Defined Benefit plans, Target Benefit plans, Defined Contribution plans, Deferred Qualified, Profit Sharing plans, Group Annuities, and Individual Policy Pension Trusts were all explored.

The results of this effort were disappointing. All of the plans considered did enjoy the advantage of being tax deductible, but they consequently had to meet the nondiscrimination requirements of such qualified plans. Since Testing Inc.'s executives make very little more than their scientist employees (Williams, for example, makes less than five of them) and since many of the employees have years of service with the company almost equal to that of the founders, there was no way to concentrate the expenditure and resulting benefits on the four owner-executives.

The tax advantage of deducting the cost held some attraction because Testing Inc. is profitable. By careful tax planning Williams has been able to keep the taxable income to under $75,000 or the 30 percent bracket for federal income taxes. However, none of these qualified plans that he had explored applied anywhere near 70 percent of the $50,000 to the benefit of the principals. Consequently, the 30 percent tax advantage was eaten up by the dispersion of available funding dollars on the wrong people.

In addition, none of the plans could respond well, if at all, to the target of a five-year funding effort with full deductibility of the $50,000 in each of those years. Another, perhaps significant tax consideration of Williams is the accumulation of surplus. Testing Inc. has never paid a dividend, and its surplus, created by retained earnings, is approaching the $250,000 maximum which may expose it to a tax penalty. However, the owners of Testing Inc. foresee the company moving into more capital-intensive operations and are anxious to keep surplus availability high.

The benefit objective for the principals is $25,000 per year (fifteen years certain) in addition to any other income sources at retirement and an equal amount to their wives for fifteen years if they should die prior to retirement.

Summary of the Planning Data

Funds available $50,000 per year for five years.

Tax posture 30 percent federal-income-tax bracket.

Benefit plan $25,000 per year retirement, $25,000 per year for fifteen years for death prior to retirement.

Name	Title	Age	Salary
Tom Colby	President	50	$49,500
Bill Colby	Vice-President of Administration	48	46,000
George Ryan	Vice-President of Research	50	46,000
Ken Williams	Treasurer	45	40,000
			$181,500

The plan can be simply summarized as it affects each employee. For example, here is the one for Ken Williams:

In consideration of your:
1. Agreement to remain with the company for fifteen more years.
2. Agreeing to not compete with the company thereafter.
3. Being available to consult with the company for an appropriate fee after your retirement.

Testing Inc. agrees to:
1. Provide you with a lifetime income starting at your age sixty-five of $25,000 per year.

2. Make at least fifteen payments of $25,000 or a total of $375,000 to you or your beneficiary.
3. Supply your family with an income of $25,000 per year for fifteen years if you should die before retirement (except suicide within two years).
4. Give you a disability income payment of $5,595 per year if you should become disabled permanently prior to age sixty, in *addition* to the retirement and/or death benefits above.[1]
5. Fund this plan with annual payments to an insurance-company-guaranteed-funding vehicle acceptable to you.

Additional Information:
1. You will pay no tax on the funds as they are being accumulated for your retirement (such as the economic-benefit tax on group life insurance over $50,000 or split-dollar plans).
2. The deferred income will be taxable to you or your beneficiary when received, except for $5,000 paid to your wife at your death.
3. The obligation for Testing Inc. to make payments as agreed is firm and irrevocable, but does not constitute a preference over other obligations.

The Obligation

The obligation that Testing Inc. undertakes here is:

Tom Colby	$25,000 for 15 years	=	$375,000
Bill Colby	$25,000 for 15 years	=	375,000
George Ryan	$25,000 for 15 years	=	375,000
Ken Williams	$25,000 for 15 years	=	375,000
			$1,500,000

These sums will be paid starting at death or at age sixty-five. Because of the life expectancy of a male at age sixty-five, no substantive difference exists between a life annuity at that age and a fifteen-year-level payout. Thus, the $375,000 is essentially correct.

Meeting the Obligation

The obligation will be met by individual insurance policies on each of these employees:

	Tax Free Inflow at Time of Death	
	Minimum Amount	*Maximum Amount*
Tom Colby	$250,000	$321,431
Bill Colby	250,000	320,635
George Ryan	250,000	321,431
Ken Williams	250,000	285,466
	$1,000,000	$1,248,963

The $1,000,000 is sufficient to meet the $1,500,000 obligation since the payments are being made over time and interest of 5.5 percent on the unpaid amounts will meet the payout schedule. The $1,000,000 is certain since all the insurance contracts are designed to be paid up before the youngest person is eligible for retirement, and each contract is paid up before that individual is retired.

Although the sufficiency of the funding is assured by the death (sooner or later) of the individuals, the availability of funds with which to meet current cash-flow obligations, should the firm be unable to do so out of its then current earnings, is an important adjunct of the plan. These funds could be provided by borrowing portions of the equity available in the paid-up policies.

The Cost

The cost of the plan is spread over the productive life of the employees and measured against the capacity of the company to meet plan costs:

Tom Colby	$15,491 for 5 years	=	$77,455
Bill Colby	14,282 for 5 years	=	71,410
George Ryan	15,491 for 5 years	=	77,455
Ken Williams	5,595 for 14 years	=	78,330
	$50,859		$304,650

That is $50,859 for five years and $5,595 for an additional nine years. The Department of Defense contract monitor responsible for the overseeing of Testing Inc.'s government contracts has determined that this amount is an "allowable" expense under their expense-reimbursement contracts and cited Defense Auditing Regulation 15 as the authority (see appendix G).

Although worst-case long-term possibilities are being met by the plan, there is a high probability that the firm will enjoy better than a worst-case situation. Of course, it is also wise to test the adequacy of the short-term cash-flow resources of the plan as well. This test has the additional benefit of avoiding the temptation to overfund.

There are several factors that would make the plan profitable to the firm. If, for example, either Tom Colby or George Ryan were to die in the first year, the proceeds of $261,692 and the savings on future annual premiums that need not be paid make the plan instantly profitable.

If the tax implications are recognized, a further area of profit is apparent. The proceeds at the time of death will be received by the firm free of taxes. That is, they will become immediately untaxed surplus. However, the payments to a retired principal or his heirs are tax deductible to the firm. The effect then, if the tax posture of the firm is unchanged, is that the $25,000 annual payments are paid with seventy-cent dollars and strike surplus as a $17,500 reduction rather than $25,000.

Finally, if a realistic rate of interest is used to discount the stream of payments, the lessened obligation also results in a gain to the firm. Making reasonable assumptions as to these three factors allows for a quantification of the value of the plan over and above its ability to meet the worst-case situations and allows a prediction of cash-flow availability.

Step 1. Define the assumptions:

Interest rate: The amount the firm earns on its capital, or at which it can borrow	14 percent
Tax rate: Federal Income Taxes	30 percent
Probability of Death:	Commissioner's Standard Mortality Table of 1958

Step 2. Calculate the net present value:

PV of the stream of fifteen $17,500 (net after-tax) payments, *PMT* using the above assumptions as to taxes and interest:

PV = present value.
i = periodic interest rate as a decimal.
N = number of compounding periods for compound-interest situations or number of payment periods for annuities situations.
PMT = periodic payment amount.

$$PV = PMT \ \frac{1 - (1+i)^{-N}}{i}$$

(Present value can also be obtained by using published tables for discounting, and a condensed but useful table is provided in appendix H.)

$$PV = \$107,487$$

Thus we conclude that $107,487 is needed at the time of death or retirement of each of the principals.

Step 3. Factor in mortality:
The funds available at the time of a death prior to retirement are obviously well in excess of the $107,487 that would be needed. A substantially lesser amount will be available if no death occurs (the cash or loan value in the policies). The probable value of this mixture of fund sources can be measured by a technique called "Investment Decisions under Uncertainty."[2] When probability factors can be assigned to the various conditions that could affect the value of the funds available at a certain time in the future, a mathematical estimate can be made. The formulas used to make these estimates are:

$$E(R) = \sum_{i=1}^{n} R_i P_i$$

and

$$\sigma_R = \sqrt{\sum_{i=1}^{n} [R_i - E(R_i)]^2 P_i}$$

where:

$E(R)$ = expected value of project return.
R_i = return for project if condition in period i exists.
P_i = probability that condition in period i will occur.
σ_R = standard deviation of expected value of return.

Note that:

$$\sqrt{\sum_{i=1}^{n} [R_i - E(R)]^2 P_i} = \sqrt{\sum_{i=1}^{n} R_i^2 P_i - \left(\sum_{i=1}^{n} P_i R_i \right)^2}$$

These rather formidable equations can be worked in easy stages where the logic is not obscurred by the mathematics. First, establish the probability of a death[3] in the next fifteen years prior to the oldest participant reaching age sixty-five.

Probability of Death prior to the Oldest Participant Reaching Sixty-Five/Fifteen Years

Using the 1958 Commissioners Standard Ordinary Mortality Table and the method described in chapter 3 the following calculation is made.

| | At Present | | In Fifteen Years | | |
	Age	Number Living	Age	Number Living	Probability of a Death
Tom Colby	50	8,762,306	65	6,800,531	0.224
Bill Colby	48	8,891,204	63	7,195,099	0.191
George Ryan	50	8,762,306	65	6,800,531	0.224
Ken Williams	45	9,048,999	60	7,698,698	0.149

Probability of one death in next fifteen years = 0.788 or 78.8 percent. Once the probability of a death for each of the participants is known, the probability of no death can be calculated by simple subtraction. A 22.4 percent probability of death means a 77.6 percent probability of no death. One also knows the dollars that would be available in either case, and an expected value can be obtained that will give the appropriate weight to each of the probable results.

Obtaining the Expected Value at Time of First Retirement			
Name	Proceeds That Would Be Paid at Death	Probability of a Death	Weighted Value of This Outcome
Tom Colby	$268,722	× 0.224 =	$60,194
Bill Colby	268,397	× 0.191 =	51,264
George Ryan	268,722	× 0.224 =	60,194
Ken Williams	280,026	× 0.149 =	41,724
		Subtotal	$213,376

	Cash or Loan Values That Would Be Available If No Death Occurs		Probability of No Death		Weighted Value of This Outcome
Tom Colby	$107,489	×	0.776	=	$83,411
Bill Colby	102,089	×	0.809	=	82,590
George Ryan	107,489	×	0.851	=	83,411
Ken Williams	96,089	×	0.851	=	81,722
The sum of all the weighted values					$331,134
is the expected value					$544,510

The formula in step 3 includes the calculation of the standard deviation of the probabilities. This provides a measure of the dispersion and an index of the degree of certainty with which the results can be expected to occur. While useful for those who can readily make that calculation, it is omitted here as unduly complex.

Step 4. Comparison of cash available with needs:

Compare the expected value of cash-flow availability with the expected value of cash-flow availability with the expected need for funds based on the assumptions as to taxes and interest:

Expected Cash Available		Funds Needed
		$107,487 per person
		× 4
$544,510	versus	$429,948

The difference between the two represents the expected profit to Testing Inc. of $114,612 and the comfort factor if the assumptions were flawed with too high an expectation of interest earnings or tax deductibility. Of course, alternative assumptions can be tested.

A further comfort factor lies in the fact that at the point of this calculation, K. Williams has five years before retirement and B. Colby two. No additional funds are being put into the plan, but the investment growth during that period, or the death of either, will swell the available funds by a minimum of $32,129.

Step 5. Funds available if no death occurs:

A further safety-net test compares the funds available at retirement age if no death occurs. The normal implementation of the plan assumes that this pre-death obligation would be funded from the firm's current earnings, but if that were not possible the firm would turn to the premortality equity available from the plan.

Name	Funds Available with No Death at Retirement Age Sixty-Five		Projected Need for Funds at Retirement
Tom Colby	107,489	versus	107,487
Bill Colby	110,926	versus	107,487
George Ryan	107,489	versus	107,487
Ken Williams	119,381	versus	107,487
	445,285		429,948

Step 6. Viewing the plan as an entity:

By repeating step 3 for those years in which retirements commence, the emerging liability can be compared with composite funding available in the two most extreme situations and the fund availability at the expected rate of mortality for those key years (see table 6-1).

Conclusion

The plan cost is approximately within the target range of Testing Inc. of $50,000 for five years with a small spillover thereafter for the youngest principal, but in any event fully funded before he reaches age sixty-one. Very importantly, all of the economic effort has been concentrated exactly where it was intended to be. The advantage of discriminatory selection is illustrated by the ability to provide K. Williams with his plan in spite of the fact that other employees have both longer service records and make more money.

The plan has taken advantage of the tax free inflow of funds inherent in the federal-tax treatment of life-insurance proceeds, bringing somewhere between $1,000,000 and $1,248,963 into surplus for a $304,650 cost. The interim (predeath) position of the firm shows the first-year cost balanced in part by a cash or loan value of $23,717 so only a net reduction in surplus of $27,142. The second year is essentially a wash, and thereafter surplus increases with each annual payment. The internalized funding has allowed a swelling of surplus by at least $400,000 before any retirement payments start.

Table 6-1
Emerging Liability Compared with Composite Funding Available

Year	Full Mortality		No Mortality		Expected Mortality
	Liability	Funds Available	Aggregate Liability as Emerging	Funds Available	Funds Available Key Years
1	$429,948	$1,035,098		$ 23,717	
2	429,948	1,077,868		72,893	
3	429,948	1,122,891		125,708	
4	429,948	1,169,388		180,555	
5	429,948	1,217,866		239,081	
6	429,948	1,190,738		254,061	
7	429,948	1,175,140		268,794	
8	429,948	1,160,943		285,307	
9	429,948	1,148,058		301,879	
10	429,948	1,136,401		318,796	
11	429,948	1,125,900		336,619	
12	429,948	1,116,530		355,633	
13	429,948	1,108,583		376,157	
14	429,948	1,102,007		400,750	
15	214,974	1,085,867	214,974	413,156	544,510
16	214,974	1,071,042		430,189	
17	107,487	1,057,534	322,461	448,079	594,681
18	107,487	1,045,255		471,575	
19	107,487	1,034,287		486,256	
20	107,487	1,024,607		507,478	
21	107,487	1,016,288		525,417	
22	107,487	1,012,521		543,471	
23	107,487	1,009,602		561,848	
24	107,487	1,006,718		580,740	
25	107,487	1,006,020	429,948	599,108	791,737

If the assumptions as to future interest rates and taxes are correct, Testing Inc. will have more than enough money and will make a profit on the plan. Similarly, in the worst-case situations where funds are needed to patch over a certain period, their availability in sufficient amounts is guaranteed. (For complete summary of the life-insurance policy funding the various plans, see tables 6-2, 6-3, and 6-4. For a summary of consolidated plan costs, see table 6-5.)

Notes

1. This benefit is equal to the amount of premium to be paid for Williams which, by contract with the insurance company, would be waived if he became disabled.

2. See Fred Weston and Eugene F. Brigham, *Managerial Finance*, 7th ed. (Hinsdale, Ill.: Dryden Press, 1981), pp. 309-316.

3. The methodology being used errs on the conservative side by assuming that a death that may be expected to have occurred during a certain period will occur at the exact end point of the period. Clearly an earlier death would produce a reduction in the amount of funding premiums that would have been paid and the addition of the investment earning on the proceeds.

Table 6-2

Summary of the Life-Insurance Policy Funding the Plan for Tom Colby and George Ryan

		Tom Colby and George Ryan, Males, Age Fifty		
Year	Premium Outlay	Policy Value Increase	Net Policy Value Year End	Death Benefit Beginning Year
1	$15,491	$ 8,013	$ 8,013	$261,692
2	15,491	15,000	23,013	275,768
3	15,491	16,203	39,216	290,519
4	15,491	16,762	55,978	305,972
5	15,491	17,865	73,844	421,431
6	0	2,971	76,815	311,905
7	0	2,727	79,541	305,918
8	0	3,236	82,777	300,250
9	0	3,008	85,786	300,250
10	0	3,044	88,830	289,787
11	0	3,356	92,185	284,961
12	0	3,494	95,680	280,413
13	0	3,885	99,565	276,209
14	0	3,770	103,335	272,322
15	0	4,154	107,489	268,722
16	0	4,302	111,792	265,387
17	0	4,464	116,256	262,315
18	0	4,659	120,915	259,507
19	0	4,882	125,797	256,989
20	0	5,396	131,193	254,779
21	0	4,580	135,773	252,912
22	0	4,480	140,253	252,132
23	0	4,594	144,847	251,534
24	0	4,691	149,539	251,071
25	0	4,521	154,059	250,722
Total	77,456	154,059		

Table 6-3
Summary of the Life-Insurance Policy Funding the Plan for Bill Colby

		Bill Colby, Male, Age Forty-Eight		
Year	*Premium Outlay*	*Policy Value Increase*	*Net Policy Value at Year End*	*Death Benefit Beginning Year*
1	$14,282	$ 7,463	$ 7,463	$261,714
2	14,282	14,085	21,548	275,674
3	14,282	14,949	36,497	290,261
4	14,282	15,684	52,181	304,660
5	14,282	16,720	68,902	320,635
6	0	2,772	71,674	310,609
7	0	2,798	74,471	304,685
8	0	3,062	77,533	299,147
9	0	3,068	80,601	293,929
10	0	3,323	83,924	288,985
11	0	3,097	87,021	284,289
12	0	3,445	90,465	279,842
13	0	3,819	94,285	275,707
14	0	3,706	97,991	271,897
15	0	4,097	102,089	268,397
16	0	4,227	106,316	265,188
17	0	4,611	110,926	262,235
18	0	4,756	115,682	259,525
19	0	4,916	120,599	257,056
20	0	5,107	125,705	254,833
21	0	4,454	130,159	252,880
22	0	4,393	134,552	251,939
23	0	4,590	139,142	251,231
24	0	4,738	143,880	250,759
25	0	4,601	148,481	250,459

Table 6-4
Summary of the Life-Insurance Policy Funding the Plan for Ken Williams

		Ken Williams, Male, Age Forty-Five		
Year	Premium Outlay	Policy Value Increase	Net Policy Value at Year End	Death Benefit Beginning Year
1	$5,595	$ 228	$ 228	$250,000
2	5,595	5,092	5,319	250,658
3	5,595	5,460	10,779	251,592
4	5,595	5,639	16,418	252,784
5	5,595	6,073	22,491	254,369
6	5,595	6,266	28,757	256,319
7	5,595	6,484	35,241	258,619
8	5,595	6,979	42,220	261,296
9	5,595	7,486	49,706	264,374
10	5,595	7,505	57,212	267,842
11	5,595	8,016	65,228	271,689
12	5,595	8,589	73,817	275,862
13	5,595	8,925	82,742	280,458
14	5,595	9,290	92,032	285,466
15	0	4,057	96,089	280,026
16	0	4,200	100,289	275,080
17	0	4,351	104,641	270,651
18	0	4,510	109,151	266,716
19	0	4,912	114,063	263,253
20	0	5,318	119,381	260,216
21	0	4,331	123,712	257,584
22	0	4,702	128,413	256,318
23	0	4,599	133,012	255,303
24	0	4,770	137,782	254,563
25	0	4,727	142,509	254,117

Table 6-5
Summary of Consolidated Plan Costs Assuming No Deaths

Year	Premium Outlay	Policy Value	Effect on Surplus	
			Current Year	Cumulative
1	$50,859	$ 23,717	$(27,142)	$ (27,142)
2	50,859	72,893	(1,683)	(28,825)
3	50,859	125,708	1,956	(26,869)
4	50,859	180,555	3,988	(22,881)
5	50,859	239,081	7,667	(15,214)
6	5,595	254,061	9,385	(5,829)
7	5,595	268,794	9,138	3,309
8	5,595	285,307	10,914	14,227
9	5,595	301,879	10,977	25,204
10	5,595	318,796	11,322	36,526
11	5,595	336,619	12,228	48,754
12	5,595	355,633	13,419	62,173
13	5,595	376,157	14,929	77,102
14	5,595	396,693	14,941	92,043
15		413,156	16,483	108,506
16		430,192	17,036	125,542
17		448,079	17,887	143,429
18		466,663	18,584	162,013
19		486,256	19,593	181,606
20		507,472	21,216	202,822
21		525,417	17,945	220,767
22		543,471	18,054	238,821
23		561,848	18,377	257,198
24		580,740	18,892	276,090
25		599,108	18,368	294,458

7 The Funding Media

The funding of Deferred Compensation has changed little over the past quarter century, except for greater flexibility that has been introduced into insurance policies that allows better fitting of the plans to the needs of the participants. Using the methodology provided in this book and the employer's concurrence with the assumptions, the appropriate level can be established and maintained for the death benefits and the safety net.

Clearly one starts with the death benefit, because the tax and funds-flow leverage in funding with mortality begins there. Most authorities feel that the individual death benefits should be close to the *undiscounted* sum of all the payments that are ultimately to be paid to that individual. This tends to make the plan *profitable* under normal conditions and assures that in a worst-case situation the plan will persist to accomplish its intended purpose. Term life insurance would, of course, provide this first objective, and in the instances where the plan extends downward to include some rather young employees whose likelihood of remaining with the firm is uncertain, this may be an appropriate answer for a period of time. However, it is an intrinsic part of the Deferred Compensation concept that it is to be funded during the productive worklife of each employee. Consequently, 100 percent of the funding for mortality should be complete by the time of the normal retirement date. This translates into some form of paid-up whole-life policy or its equivalent.

Any paid-up policy will have significant cash values, and they provide the solid framework of the safety net. The intensity with which that framework needs to be reinforced (if at all) will dictate the type of policy, side funding, accelerated premium, etcetera, which should be employed. If normal retirement is fairly late, that is, after age sixty-five, and if assumptions as to taxes and interest are not too conservative, supplemental funding of the safety net will probably not be required.

One relatively new concept that accommodates many of the requirements of Deferred Compensation plans is that of the *vanishing premium*. By restructuring the use of dividends, the premium-paying period can be shortened without suffering the adverse tax consequences of discounting future premiums. The use of this concept has the further advantage of being open-ended on the upside since the premium crossover point does not mean that additional premiums could not be paid. Therefore, if it is judged the safety net needs enrichment, that can be done.

43

The basic idea of vanishing premiums is that premiums are paid until dividends can fund the payments of future years. Technically, dividends are used to buy paid-up additions. At the crossover year (the year in which the cash value of the paid-up additions can completely fund the contract) the cash value of current paid-up additions plus the value of future additions will begin to be surrendered to pay future premiums.

By adding units of an annual premium-increasing-insurance rider (APIIR) as offered by some participating (mutual) companies, the vanishing point can be shortened or tailored to fit any situation based on age and need. In the case of Testing Inc. this technique was used to address the firm's objective of a $50,000 annual outlay for a five-year period. William's rather small premium vanished in fourteen years. By adding APIIR premium outlay for the Colby brothers and Ryan it was shortened to five years.

By continuing to pay premiums after the vanishing point two things occur. First, total cash available will grow dramatically, and second, the death benefit will expand at a rate far greater than premium outlay. In short, the plan has a built-in valve to ease the pressures of inflation. All that is needed is to continue payments and update the agreement. All the components necessary for an expanded plan for existing participants are in place. Finally, making payments beyond the vanishing point will reinforce the safety net by providing additional funds for living benefits until mortality strikes.

Life with premiums to age sixty-five, or sometimes seventy, has been commonly selected, particularly where a nonparticipation (stock-insurance company) product is used. Some of the emerging products that respond to shorter-term interest rates such as Current Assumption life or Universal life may prove to be useful. Clearly both the mortality portion and the safety-net portion need to be acquired in a cost-effective way. Once the assumptions have been made and the plan design fixed, a competent professional underwriter should have no difficulty in fitting a product or products to the task.

8

Several Layers of Benefit and a Nonprofit Organization

A nonprofit organization might be regarded as a poor candidate for a mortality-funded Deferred Compensation plan since the advantages of receipt of the face amount of the life-insurance policy (and the deductibility of the payments to the recipients) does not have the same leverage it would have with an ordinary business. However, a qualified plan suffers a similar loss of leverage. In those instances where the institution does not have Social Security, there is an absence of benefits that threatens the ability of the institution to get and keep quality employees. Deferred Compensation offers the opportunity to solve this issue in a creative way by tying good professionals to the institution and providing meaningful benefits. The selective determination of eligibility and vesting keeps costs within reach.

Bristol Business College was acquired by Ed Reynolds and Phil Turner in 1968. Nine years later the pressure from competitors who paid neither income, real estate, nor sales taxes forced a decision to seek reorganization as a tax-exempt 501(c)3 organization. This successful transition became the turning point, and the moderately successful college became substantially more successful in contrast to the current trend of institutions of higher learning.

Four years ago they were able to attract a capable financial manager, John Bailey, as the bursar. Shortly thereafter Dr. Vincent Carpenter was brought aboard as academic dean. These two, together with Robert Jones, dean of students, form a team who are informally being groomed as successor management.

The trustees of the college are naturally pleased that their managers have dealt so well with the difficult issues confronting colleges. They have three major concerns. First, they see an obligation to build some security for Reynolds and Turner who not only lost their proprietary interest but made substantial investments of both effort and direct-capital contribution. They not only kept their salaries very low but also sold to the college several buildings which they owned at cost. The second objective is to assure the college of continued excellence of managerial skills and academic proficiency by keeping not only Reynolds and Turner, but also those of the senior staff essential to the continued success of the college. The trustees had reached a gentlemen's agreement with Reynolds and Turner that some kind of retirement plan would be in place and funded by the time they reached fifty-five, at which time it was expected that those being groomed to take over would be able to do so. The final objective was to begin to solve the problem of permanent employees not covered by Social Security (as employees of many institutions are not).

Opting out of the Social Security program had an effect on the success of the college because it obviously represented a savings of approximately 6 percent of the college's entire payroll, or more like 13 percent if the contributions of both the employees and the college are counted. As there were no employees close to age sixty-two, the limited resources available were directed to the concerns of disability income and in a modest way to premature deaths with a solid program of Long Term Disability and some Group Term life insurance. The usual tax-sheltered investment vehicles, which are available to educational institutions, were made available on a voluntary basis, but the success of that part of the employee benefit program was very limited.

An analysis of the longer term implications of meeting all three objectives determined that an annual economic effort of $90,000 would be required. In today's dollars this was still substantially less than the Social Security would have cost the college alone and did not count the matching contribution that would be required by employees. A decision was made to undertake this funding in stages. The upcoming budget was built to include $35,000 to $40,000 for stage one. It was recognized that the college's healthy income position would not preclude heavy bank borrowings between tuition inflows. Using a stage-up system would allow the policy cash value to trickle back onto the balance sheet and give sufficient ballast to assure that loans would be granted. Then the next stage could be undertaken.

Summary of Stage One Planning Data

Earnings assumption	16 percent
Funds available	$37,500 per year
Tax posture	Not applicable
Benefit plan	Top executives Reynolds and Turner 50 percent of salary Others 25 percent of salary Benefits payable for life (fifteen years certain) upon retirement at age sixty-five, or for fifteen years upon death prior to retirement
Vesting	Sum of age and service to equal seventy

Name	Title	Age Now	Age When Vested	Salary	Benefit
Reynolds	President	48	52	$62,500	$31,250
Turner	Provost	45	51	62,500	31,250
Bailey	Bursar	50	58	40,900	10,225
Jones	Dean	45	51	41,250	10,313
Carpenter	Dean	46	56	36,000	9,000
				$243,150	

The first effort involved getting a fix on the total funds that would ultimately be needed and establishing a level for the safety net based on the assumptions provided by the college. As there was no tax leverage to be applied, this only involved the calculation for the net present value of the stream of income payments. Since the ages of all participants were clustered together, it was determined to focus on the first retirement as the key emerging liability.

	Fifteen Years of Payments to Participants		
	Benefit	Aggregate	Net Present Value at 16 Percent Interest
Reynolds	$32,500	$487,500	$181,202
Turner	32,500	487,500	181,202
Bailey	10,225	153,375	57,009
Jones	10,313	154,895	57,499
Carpenter	9,000	135,000	50,179
	$94,538	$1,296,570	$527,091

It then remained to find a mortality-funding plan that would fit the objectives of meeting the ultimate liability with mortality proceeds and having a safety net with the expected value in fifteen years of $527,091. The probability of one death within the fifteen years was calculated:

	Probability of Death before Oldest Participant Reaches Sixty-five (Fifteen Years)			
Age	Number Living	Age	Number Living	Probability of Death
50	8,762,306	65	6,800,531	22.39%
48	8,891,204	63	7,195,099	19.08
45	9,048,999	60	7,698,698	14.92
45	9,048,999	60	7,698,698	14.92
46	9,000,587	61	7,542,106	16.20
Probability of one death:				87.51%

The funding illustrated by table 8-1 met the several objectives: (1) ultimately funded by mortality on policies fully paid up during the working life of the participants (a range of $1,070,000 to $1,169,730 in the next fifteen years resulting from the use of paid-up additions against an ultimate liability of $1,296,570); (2) a safety net of $553,758 against an emerging liability of $527,091; (3) a premium under $37,500; and (4) full payment of the policies on Reynolds and Turner by the time that they will have reached age fifty-five.

Periodic Review

After one year the college continued to prosper and consideration was given to both the general soundness of the plan and the possibility of extending the original effort to embrace more of the long-term goals. The routine review found the college officials somewhat less optimistic about their prior year's interest assumption of 16 percent and consequently less satisfied about the margin of safety designed into the safety net. As expected, the flow back to the balance sheet of the first-year cash values of $9,456 and the expected cash value for the second year of $42,392 meant that the college surplus was not suffering an erosion that would impair its borrowing power. The revised view of the interest earnings at 12 percent was calculated:

	Fifteen Years of Payments to Participants	
	Annual Benefit	*Net Present Value at 12 Percent Interest*
Reynolds	$32,500	$221,353
Turner	32,500	221,353
Bailey	10,225	69,641
Jones	10,313	70,240
Carpenter	9,000	61,297
		$643,884
The expected value in 15 years		553,758
Shortfall		$ 90,126

Thus the first measure to be taken would be to enrich the safety net by the $90,126.

Table 8-1
Deferred Compensation Summary for Bristol Business College

Name	Age	Insurance Amount	Annual Premium	Premium Payment Period	Fifteenth Year Cash Value	Fifteenth Year Death Benefit	Probability of Death	Anticipated Cash to Bristol Business College[a]
Reynolds	48	$ 410,000	$18,110	7 years	$167,362	$ 440,109	19.1%	$219,457
Turner	45	360,000	10,553	10 years	135,509	385,375	14.9%	172,739
Bailey	50	100,000	3,006	13 years	43,573	114,334	22.4%	59,423
Jones	45	100,000	2,341	14 years	38,421	114,242	14.9%	49,718
Carpenter	46	100,000	2,459	14 years	40,194	115,670	16.2%	52,421
Total:		1,070,000	36,469		425,059	1,169,730	87.5%	553,758

[a]Probability of death times death benefit + probability of living times cash value.

The priorities for the next stage of expansion of the plan included adding $10,000 to the annual benefit of Jones, Bailey, and Carpenter and extending the plan downward to pick up seven additional people. Inasmuch as those seven were all ages forty or under, it was fairly obvious that their inclusion in the plan would help address the shortfall in the emerging liability because mortality proceeds or interim cash values would increase the available funds.

The increase to the top three was addressed first. Using a $150,000 face-value life-insurance policy for each covered the entire undiscounted future obligation. The net present value of $10,000 per year for fifteen years was calculated at $68,108 for each participant using the more conservative 12-percent-interest figure. The total of the three constitute a goal for the safety net of $204,325. Using the system for weighting results based on their probability of happening, a forecast of expected results fourteen years hence was made:

	No Death Cash Value	Death Proceeds	Expected Value
Jones	$60,258	$173,444	$ 78,594
Bailey	60,314	163,064	83,330
Carpenter	58,500	167,532	77,690
			$239,614

Thus the safety net was improved by this increase in benefits by the difference between the added obligation discounted at 12 percent, or $204,325, and the added expected value of $239,614, or $35,289. The premium outlay for this plan increase was $12,267. (The growth of the death proceeds in fourteen years to more than $150,000 is explained by using the dividends to buy paid-up additions.)

The college wished to proceed cautiously in the amount of funds it was locking up into reserves for Deferred Compensation but was anxious to tie in the additional seven people whose average income was $30,000 and offset the absence of Social Security benefits for them. The oldest of the seven was forty, so no retirements were to be expected from the group for at least twenty-five years. Consequently, it was considered not imprudent to defer establishing a safety net until they individually reached age forty-five and to only confront the contractual liability of premature death by funding this for the interim period with term life insurance. This deferral posed no barrier to engaging in a Deferred Compensation agreement with each employee exactly like those that had been given to the senior staff. This agreement covered both preretirement death and full retirement benefits, except that each agreement provided only $15,000 per year for ten years certain. Looking at the entire network of agreements, Reynolds was able to see that the Deferred Compensation funding plan had incidentally provided him with a buffer of cash against the loss by death of any of his key people. The impact on the safety net was similarly positive:

Name	Age	Mortality Amount	Probability of Death	Expected Value
\multicolumn{5}{c}{*The Addition to the Safety Net by Adding a Death-Only Funding for Junior People*}				

The Addition to the Safety Net by Adding a
Death-Only Funding for Junior People

Name	Age	Mortality Amount	Probability of Death	Expected Value
Andrews	40	$150,000	9.8%	$14,700
Burns	28	150,000	4.0	6,000
Costello	35	150,000	6.5	9,750
DiCarlo	34	150,000	6.0	9,000
Epstein	32	150,000	5.2	7,800
Greim	34	150,000	6.0	9,000
Hadley	30	150,000	4.6	6,900
				$74,700

Because of the youth of this group it added only $1,459 to the premium outlay. The shortfall that developed by revision of the interest rate to 12 percent, $90,126, had been overcome by the $35,289 attributable to the improved benefits for Bailey, Jones, and Carpenter and the $74,700 from the death-only plan (a total of $109,989). A death in the death-only plan would, of course, produce a concomitant expense. That impact is much diminished by the discounted value of the funds flow and the near certainty that most payments to participants' beneficiaries would not have been paid at the end of the period.

In this two-stage effort Bristol Business College has effectively dealt with the needs of twelve of its key people. The annual incurred cost of $50,195 or 11 percent of *their* pay (and 2.7 percent of the total college payroll) is well within its budget and far below the cost of Social Security. The plan is selective and tailored to the real needs: high retirement benefits for the two founders funded by the time they reach age fifty-five and an array of benefits for junior staffers that meets their needs. The incurred costs essentially leave the college's surplus unreduced because the funding is internalized, and a funds availability for loss of a key person is a corollary benefit. (For specific examples of Deferred Compensation plans, see tables 8-2, 8-3, 8-4, 8-5, and 8-6.)

Table 8-2
Benefit Plan for Ed Reynolds
Male, current age forty-eight
LP 95 nonsmoker
Face amount: $410,000
Annual premium: $17,360
Annual premium increasing insurance rider: 67.4550 units
Dividends to purchase paid-up additions

Policy Year	Proposed Annual Outlay	Annual Illustrated Dividend	Guaranteed Cash Value	Cash Value of Dividend Additions	Total Cash Value	Paid-up Dividend Additions	Net Insurance Death Benefit
1	$17,360	$ 750	$ 5,963	$ 838	$ 6,801	$ 2,267	$420,088
2	17,360	910	21,474	2,015	23,489	5,276	433,196
3	17,360	1,078	37,678	3,550	41,227	9,003	446,742
4	17,360	1,374	54,165	5,602	59,767	13,768	460,760
5	17,360	1,693	71,359	8,223	79,582	19,593	475,656
6	17,360	2,017	88,863	11,448	100,311	26,455	491,496
7	17,360	2,333	106,691	15,312	122,004	34,337	508,331
8	0	2,628	118,602	8,399	127,001	18,288	493,953
9	0	2,907	128,379	3,768	132,147	7,969	481,947
10	0	3,186	133,659	3,936	137,595	8,091	473,882
11	0	3,493	138,504	4,167	142,671	8,330	466,180
12	0	3,920	143,800	4,517	148,317	8,786	458,885
13	0	4,383	149,672	4,907	154,579	9,292	452,101
14	0	4,854	155,348	5,308	160,656	9,792	445,850
15	0	5,318	161,668	5,704	167,372	10,258	440,109
16	0	5,752	168,226	6,076	174,302	10,657	434,843
17	0	6,179	175,417	6,443	181,860	11,029	429,998
18	0	6,613	182,834	6,821	189,655	11,404	425,549
19	0	7,060	190,499	7,216	197,715	11,790	421,497
20	0	7,540	198,438	7,647	206,085	12,221	417,848

Table 8-3
Benefit Plan for Phil Turner

Male, current age forty-five
LP 95 nonsmoker
Face amount: $360,000
Annual premium: $10,150
Annual premium increasing insurance rider: 20.9340 units
Dividends to purchase paid-up additions

Policy Year	Proposed Annual Outlay	Annual Illustrated Dividend	Guaranteed Cash Value	Cash Value of Dividend Additions	Total Cash Value	Paid-up Dividend Additions	Net Insurance Death Benefit
1	$10,150	$ 328	$ 1,851	$ 356	$ 2,206	$ 1,063	$363,514
2	10,150	475	10,832	918	11,750	2,654	368,312
3	10,150	619	20,262	1,696	21,958	4,742	373,491
4	10,150	842	29,779	2,781	32,560	7,523	379,034
5	10,150	1,058	39,748	4,183	43,931	10,954	385,157
6	10,150	1,274	49,814	5,919	55,733	15,012	391,838
7	10,150	1,512	59,981	8,031	68,011	19,736	399,083
8	10,150	1,771	70,612	10,560	81,171	25,160	406,966
9	10,150	2,030	81,711	13,531	95,243	31,270	415,527
10	10,150	2,286	92,562	16,965	109,527	38,044	424,773
11	0	2,520	101,823	12,288	114,111	26,754	414,330
12	0	2,826	111,483	7,684	119,168	16,252	404,445
13	0	3,132	120,812	3,556	124,368	7,310	395,630
14	0	3,460	125,860	3,823	129,683	7,642	390,300
15	0	3,798	131,401	4,108	135,509	7,991	385,375
16	0	4,169	137,101	4,428	141,529	8,385	380,847
17	0	4,540	143,002	4,751	147,753	8,765	376,737
18	0	4,907	149,115	5,074	154,189	9,124	373,025
19	0	5,252	155,808	5,379	161,186	9,434	369,693
20	0	5,591	163,071	5,679	168,750	9,722	366,703

54

Deferred Compensation

Table 8-4
Funding of Benefit Plan for John Bailey

Age	Policy Year	At Start of Year		At End of Year	
		Annual Outlay	Cumulative Financial Outlay	Net Equity	Net Death Benefit
50	1	$2,871	$ 2,871	$ 209	$100,514
51	2	2,871	5,742	2,681	101,146
52	3	2,871	8,613	5,425	101,907
53	4	2,871	11,484	8,174	102,858
54	5	2,871	14,355	11,133	103,992
55	6	2,871	17,226	14,300	105,287
56	7	2,871	20,097	17,475	106,732
57	8	2,871	22,968	20,965	108,325
58	9	2,871	25,839	24,479	110,074
59	10	2,871	28,710	28,129	111,985
60	11	2,871	31,581	32,029	114,073
61	12	2,871	34,452	36,114	116,390
62	13	2,871	37,323	40,492	118,929
63	14	0	37,323	41,954	116,527
64	15	0	37,323	43,573	114,334
65	17	0	37,323	45,255	112,345
66	17	0	37,323	47,007	110,559
67	18	0	37,323	48,843	108,982
68	19	0	37,323	50,774	107,621
69	20	0	37,323	52,917	106,484
70	21	0	37,323	54,741	105,954

Note: John Bailey age fifty; $100,000 life paid up at ninety-five; dividends used to buy additions with premium offset.

Table 8-5
Funding of Benefit Plan for Robert Jones

Age	Policy Year	At Start of Year Annual Outlay	At Start of Year Cumulative Financial Outlay	At End of Year Net Equity	At End of Year Net Death Benefit
45	1	$2,253	$ 2,253	$ 91	$100,263
46	2	2,253	4,506	2,128	100,637
47	3	2,253	6,759	4,312	101,114
48	4	2,253	9,012	6,567	101,748
49	5	2,253	11,265	8,997	102,528
50	6	2,253	13,518	11,503	103,448
51	7	2,253	15,771	14,097	104,519
52	8	2,253	18,024	16,888	105,750
53	9	2,253	20,277	19,883	107,138
54	10	2,253	22,530	22,885	108,676
55	11	2,253	24,783	26,091	110,345
56	12	2,253	27,036	29,527	112,184
57	13	2,253	29,289	33,098	114,188
58	14	2,253	31,542	36,814	116,366
59	15	0	31,542	38,421	114,242
60	16	0	31,542	40,084	112,331
61	17	0	31,542	41,807	110,623
62	18	0	31,542	43,593	109,108
63	19	0	31,542	45,539	107,770
64	20	0	31,542	47,646	106,597
65	21	0	31,542	49,358	105,977
66	22	0	31,542	51,217	105,461
67	23	0	31,542	53,034	105,059
68	24	0	31,542	54,919	104,778
69	25	0	31,542	56,785	104,634
70	26	0	31,542	58,737	104,622

Note: Robert Jones age forty-five; $100,000 life paid up at ninety-five; dividends used to buy additions with premium offset.

Table 8-6
Funding of Benefit Plan for Vince Carpenter

Age	Policy Year	At Start of Year		At End of Year	
		Annual Outlay	Cumulative Financial Outlay	Net Equity	Net Death Benefit
46	1	$2,364	$ 2,364	$ 149	$100,417
47	2	2,364	4,728	2,344	100,931
48	3	2,364	7,092	4,586	101,535
49	4	2,364	9,456	6,999	102,280
50	5	2,364	11,820	9,487	103,163
51	6	2,364	14,184	12,161	104,195
52	7	2,364	16,548	14,929	105,382
53	8	2,364	18,912	17,898	106,724
54	9	2,364	21,276	20,973	108,214
55	10	2,364	23,640	24,149	109,833
56	11	2,364	26,004	27,529	111,570
57	12	2,364	28,368	31,040	113,472
58	13	2,364	30,732	34,693	115,547
59	14	2,364	33,096	38,600	117,801
60	15	0	33,096	40,194	115,670
61	16	0	33,096	41,845	113,748
62	17	0	33,096	43,654	112,021
63	18	0	33,096	45,518	110,474
64	19	0	33,096	47,439	109,094
65	20	0	33,096	49,521	107,878
66	21	0	33,096	51,315	107,215
67	22	0	33,096	53,061	106,664
68	23	0	33,096	54,870	106,235
69	24	0	33,096	56,756	105,941
70	25	0	33,096	58,620	105,776

Note: Vince Carpenter aged forty-six; $100,000 life paid up at ninety-five; dividends used to buy additions with premium offset.

Ralph Emerson:
A One-Man Case

This case may appear to be somewhat out of the main stream of Deferred Compensation plans, dealing as it does with someone already receiving retirement and Social Security benefits. However, it illustrates some elements that might be of value as adjuncts in other plans; the key man aspect; and a method of dealing with the principal who is already sixty-five and inching into retirement.

The Problem

Ralph Emerson approached his sixty-fifth birthday with mixed emotions. He had long looked forward to an easing of some of the pressures and demands that were associated with his role as sales manager of the northeast region for his company, but he dreaded lapsing into total inactivity. His financial position was secure, if modest, since the company at normal retirement date would supply him with a pension which, together with social security, would aggregate 60 percent of his current earnings. With a lesser tax this would provide a very livable, though diminished, net spendable income. The loss of a company car, entertainment allowance, and other perks further reduced the standard at which he would live, but that would be balanced by the inactivity about which he was apprehensive.

The top management of Ralph's company was also viewing Ralph's retirement with misgivings. Due to a recent series of unplanned corporate changes, a successor was not in place to take over the reins as Ralph reached sixty-five. If Ralph could be persuaded to remain in his position as northeast sales manager on a reduced schedule, it would be possible to find and groom his replacement.

The barriers to simply continuing Ralph's employment were several. Ralph could not earn over $7,500 per year after retirement without giving up substantial Social Security benefits, and he understandably felt that if he were to continue to hold the major responsibility for the northeast he should be suitably rewarded. The company could also foresee that by leaving a sixty-five-year old in such a key position they were vulnerable to a loss of direct bottom line profits due to his premature death or a loss due to the expenses associated with an abrupt, inconvenient replacement.

After some study, a Deferred Compensation plan was worked out that overcame the barriers, and left both parties in a better financial position over the short and long term. Ralph was offered a program that included a five-year contract for employment with a reduced level of activities and obligations. His salary, which had been $50,000, would be composed of two parts: $7,500 annually in cash, and a Deferred Compensation plan that would pay $20,000 per year upon his reaching age seventy, with ten years certain, or $20,000 per year for ten years if he should die prior to age seventy. In addition, he would retain the full range of perks that he had been enjoying which included a company car, entertainment allowance, medical and dental insurance for his family, a large private office, secretarial services, telephone, postage, and other benefits, which were valued at $12,500 per year. As a result, the progression of Ralph's net disposable income from the time of his active full-time employment until his period of full retirement was made to be much smoother than he had been expecting.

| | Planned Income Stream for Ralph Emerson | | |
	Pre-retirement	Age Sixty-five to Age Seventy	After Age Seventy
Salary in cash	$50,000	$ 7,500	
Retirement and Social Security payments		30,000	$30,000
Perks	12,500	12,500	
Deferred Compensation			20,000
Allowance for taxes	9,000	1,000	2,000
Net disposable income and perks	$53,500	$49,000	$48,000

The company's concerns (apart from solving the staffing shortfall) required a flexible plan that would provide cash availability to meet both predictable and contingent obligations. If Ralph were to die before his employment contract ran out, they wanted the knowledge that any further obligations to his family were behind them and, in addition, that there would be a bulge of cash to hurry in a replacement and/or to pump into *profit* to offset the earnings dip which might result from Ralph's absence. Translated into financial terms this established several objectives:

1. The current expenditure for Ralph's reduced services should be somewhat less than for his full-time services, including the accrual for the deferred income.
2. The plan should provide a preretirement tax-free death fund which would meet any one of these tests:

a. Enough money to pay Ralph's family the $20,000 per year for ten years assuming no tax leverage and some absolutely safe level of interest such as 8 percent.
b. Enough money to pay Ralph's family the $20,000 assuming the current tax advantage of the company in the 46 percent tax bracket and a conservative rate of interest such as 12 percent; plus a spill-over to net profit of about $75,000 to balance the possible loss of business.
c. A funds flow at death that would meet the first year obligation to Ralph's family and upwards of $100,000 with which to recruit, rearrange, and force success upon the northeast region.
3. The retirement obligation to Ralph should be fully funded during the five years starting at his age sixty-five, assuming the current tax posture of the company and its ability to earn 12 percent on its investments. This should be confirmed by the availability of funds with which to immediately purchase an annuity for age seventy, ten years certain, for the expected after-tax expenditure of $10,800 per year.
4. The company should retain options to maintain high levels of life-insurance protection should Ralph's health become suspect.
5. Given that all of the above criteria can be met, the business decision will be made depending upon the objective probability that the company's financial position will be better than these minimum requirements.

Solving the Problem

Quantifying the various parameters that the company has defined:

1. The annual cost of the plan for each of the five years must be less than the $50,000 current salary, minus the amount paid in cash, or $7,500, thus less than $ 42,500.
2. Preretirement death fund tax free:

a. $20,000 for ten years @ 8 percent		= $134,200.
b. $10,800 for 10 years @ 12 percent	= 61,022	
Plus spill-over required	= +75,000	
	136,022	= $136,022.
c. First year payment to family	20,000	
Additional funds flow	100,000	
	120,000	= $120,000.

3. A minimum equity after five years in the plan equal to the cost of a life annuity for a male age seventy with ten years certain paying $10,800 annually, $63,650, or the net present

value of $10,800 per year for ten years at 12 precent, that is,
$61,022, whichever is greater   = $ 63,650.
4. A policy offering the minimum values expressed above
    which would be fully paid up at age seventy, but with the   = whole
    option to continue payments and enjoy a larger face value   life or
                                                                     similar.

The four objectives can be easily translated by a life underwriter to
mean: whole life or similar policy with a face value of greater than
$136,000, which would be paid up for at least that amount in five years and
with a cash or loan value after the fifth year of at least $61,002. A somewhat
larger face value is desired that could be maintained after age seventy by
continuing to pay premiums, and the premiums should be as low as possible, but in any event less than $42,500.

Once the policy or policies have been found that will meet these objectives
the fifth step can be undertaken. That is the weighing of the cost/benefit relationship that allows the making of a decision. Here the mixture of the probability of death or no death can be factored into the decision. To the degree
that an acceptable cost produces all of the minimum requirements and might
be expected to exceed them, the project is increasingly profitable.

In the particular solution illustrated at the end of this chapter the
minimums are only narrowly met. This has the advantage of producing the
lowest up-front cost—$17,783—which is very dramatically below the target
of $42,500. The concomitant disadvantage is that the upside gain by the
company is similarly limited. Other solutions, using a somewhat larger cost
but still within the guidelines, would produce a reinforced safety net and a
greater gain by the company if its assumptions were realized. This would be
particularly so if the extra costs were used to increase the mortality aspect of
the plan.

The implication that the company might wish to buy an annuity at
Ralph's age seventy may be important. The strategy that would usually
work best would be borrowing out the necessary funds and preserving the
tax leverage which would leave the paid-up policy in force until it matures at
death. The minimum depositing would produce a tax-deductible interest
payment since the payment of four of the first seven payments in cash has
been met. The corresponding annual increase in cash value would nearly
balance the interest payments—more than balance it, if the tax deductibility
is considered.

The calculation for the expected value of the plan to be measured
against the minimum value needed is now familiar. The cumulative value of
more than one possibility of death is missing, and the expectation that one

single event might conform to the norm is remote. Nevertheless, business decisions which always track with known probabilities will produce profitable results over time. (See table 9-1 for summary of Ralph Emerson's benefit plan.)

Probability of a death within five years:
Number living at age sixty-five   6,800,531
Number living at age seventy   5,592,012

$$1,208,519 \div 6,800,531 = 17.8$$

Calculation of expected value:
 .178 probability of $186,366 = $ 33,173
 .882 probability of $ 76,942 = $ 67,872
1.000 expected value   = $101,045
          versus
minimum value $ 61,022

Table 9-1
Life Paid Up at Ninety-Five—Vanish Premium at Seventy Using Annual Premium Increasing Insurance Rider
Prepared for Ralph Emerson
Male, current age sixty-five
Dividends: additions through year twenty-five

Year	Premium Outlay	Policy Value Increase	Difference Plus or Minus	Guaranteed Cash Value	Cash Value of Additions Year End	Net Policy Value Year End	Death Benefit Beginning Year
1	17,782	9,589	-8,193	8,543	1,046	9,589	129,664
2	17,782	15,404	-2,377	22,513	2,481	24,993	142,969
3	17,782	16,342	-1,440	36,998	4,337	41,335	155,855
4	17,782	17,292	-490	51,894	6,733	58,628	170,272
5	17,782	18,315	533	67,219	9,723	76,942	186,366
6	0	981	981	73,320	4,603	77,923	180,047
7	0	961	961	75,727	3,157	78,884	175,536
8	0	1,003	1,003	76,568	3,320	79,888	171,814
9	0	1,032	1,032	77,453	3,466	80,919	168,219
10	0	1,043	1,043	78,368	3,595	81,962	164,715
11	0	924	924	79,174	3,712	82,886	161,272
12	0	1,002	1,002	79,982	3,906	83,888	157,869
13	0	1,216	1,216	80,990	4,115	85,104	154,587
14	0	1,090	1,090	81,856	4,338	86,194	151,441
15	0	1,226	1,226	82,841	4,580	87,420	148,451
16	0	1,389	1,389	83,967	4,842	88,809	145,641
17	0	1,456	1,456	85,143	5,123	90,266	143,035
18	0	1,750	1,750	86,634	5,382	92,016	140,655
19	0	1,912	1,912	88,305	5,623	93,928	138,481
20	0	2,152	2,152	90,265	5,815	96,080	136,497

21	0	1,553	1,553	91,269	6,364	97,633	134,654
22	0	1,538	1,538	92,774	6,397	99,171	133,335
23	0	1,504	1,504	94,263	6,411	100,675	132,007
24	0	1,587	1,587	95,837	6,425	102,262	130,649
25	0	1,762	1,762	97,492	6,531	104,023	129,257
	88,909	104,023	15,114				

Note: Premiums are paid by surrendering paid-up additions beginning year six. Annual loan interest rate = 7.40 percent in advance.

[a]Includes: Dividend additions.

10 Balance Sheet, Income Statement, and Cash Flow

Inverted Accounting

It is not the purpose of this book to replace essential professional accounting assistance for any firm. However, knowledgeable managers and practitioners in the financial-planning field may find an overview of the accounting and bookkeeping will strengthen their understanding of Deferred Compensation and its applications.

A major purpose of using mortality funding for Deferred Compensation is that it has great tax advantages. The rather obvious advantage of avoiding tax when the recipient's income is at its peak and pushing some income into retirement years when a lesser tax will be payable appears to need no further explanation or examples. The problem area is accounting and bookkeeping within the firm. The tax advantages seem to make the accounting run contrary to the way in which one normally understands profits, losses, income, and expenses. For example:

> The annual amount that is set aside to meet a future obligation, such as a sinking fund to retire a debenture, would normally be a current-period expense. In Deferred Compensation the amount being set aside may indeed be an expense, but it is not a tax-deductible expense.

> A payment to a retired employee under a Deferred Compensation plan is not an expense in accounting terms if the obligation has been funded during the working life of the employee. However, the payment does give rise to a tax deduction. Consequently, the firm enjoys a tax deduction without the associated expense being charged to its operations.

> When the cash value of a policy being used to fund Deferred Compensation exceeds the premium, as it very often does after the first year in Deferred Compensation, an income or gain results which should be bookkept. However, this income or gain is not taxable as long as the policy remains in force.

> When a death occurs the cash received from the insurance company may add a very substantial amount to the firm's income. However, this income is not subject to income or capital gains tax but goes untaxed into surplus, thus improving the firm's retained earnings or allowing dividends to the owners.

These seeming anomalies are, of course, great advantages that are used in funding Deferred Compensation with mortality.

Accruing the Costs

One important issue on the income statement is how to treat, in the current period, the future obligation due to a Deferred Compensation recipient. The American Institute of Certified Public Accountants' handbook, *AICPA Professional Standards,* is somewhat ambiguous on this issue. Several sections of that handbook (sections 4063 and 4064) deal with accounting for the cost of pension plans and indicate that, in some situations, Deferred Compensation contracts should be treated as a pension plan. The situations are defined as those in which the "Deferred Compensation contracts if such contracts taken together are equivalent to a pension plan."[1] Paragraph 157 of section 4063 goes on to say that "this will not apply in many instances where Deferred Compensation contracts exist, but auditors may need to investigate this type carefully."[2] The accounting procedures for pension plans include the kinds of actuarial evaluation, with its allowances for turnover, use of pooled funding vehicles, and so on, commonly found in IRS qualified and ERISA supervised group pensions.

As there are many types of Deferred Compensation plans it is perilous to generalize. However, the type of plans that are considered in this text are largely discriminatory and selective, and they intentionally escape ERISA by being applicable to a "select group of management or highly paid employees."[3] For this reason most authorities will elect to treat these plans under the guidelines below and not as a pension plan. This accounting posture does not fly in the face of the entity concept as expressed in examples in this book. That concept simply illustrates how the assets, which are being generated in a policy on the life of one employee, can be contemplated as nourishing the security of the other plan participants and the firm, since those assets necessarily remain the unrestricted property of the firm, and no employee may have a separable interest in any portion.

The distinction as to whether a Deferred Compensation plan is a pension plan or not concerns itself only with the methodology of dealing with the liability for the future payments being accrued in the current period. The pension method may be thought of as a bulk method, and the Deferred Compensation method as an individual one. The language relative to the individual method is found in section 4064.01.

The Board believes that other Deferred Compensation contracts should be accounted for individually on an accrual basis. Such contracts customarily include certain requirements such as continued employment for a specified period and availability for consulting services and agreements not to compete after retirement, which, if not complied with remove the employer's obligation for future payments. The estimated amounts to be paid under each contract should be accrued in a systematic and rational manner over the period of active employment from the time the contract is entered into, unless it is evident that future services expected to be received by the employer are commensurate with the payments or a portion of the payments to be made.[4]

That section is further footnoted:

The amounts to be accrued periodically should result in an accrued amount which is not less than the then present value of the estimated payments to be made.[5]

The annual premium payments toward a well-constructed mortality-funded Deferred Compensation plan, in which the assumptions for the safety net are reasonable, may be the appropriate index of the amount to be accrued in the current period. This is not to say that other indices could not be found, but it is the one used in the bookkeeping examples. That section of the (CPA) handbook also allows room to defer accrual when the contingency is remote, as in the instances where this book has illustrated funding for only the preretirement death of an employee many years away from retirement. In those cases the term-insurance-premium cost would be the appropriate period cost. Similarly, there is room in the language to incur an expense greater than the amount being isolated or when nothing is being isolated (such as when the employer demurs on the annual funding, uses unreasonable assumptions for the safety net, or postpones the accumulation for some reason).

Excess Accumulation of Surplus
and Other Accrual Ideas

Where a contractual obligation exists to provide an employee with a retirement income, the accumulation of surplus to meet this obligation is not subject to 531 penalty taxes. Mortality-funded Deferred Compensation plans, with lower costs and lower accumulation of predeath surplus relative to the benefits promised, take a lesser advantage of this point than do traditionally funded plans. If sheltering of surplus from this tax is important to the firm, it may be prudent to raise the safety net or use an accrual of the liability more in line with the traditional plans. Specialized tax advice is suggested to deal with this element properly. Those firms working on a cost-plus basis may also wish to inspect concepts in which a higher accrual would be more rewarding. This strategy will be familiar to those working with qualified plans where the lowest possible assumptions are used as to interest, turnover, and mortality, which produces a higher cost and thus a higher tax deduction. Again professional assistance is recommended to avoid an unallowable cost.

The other items that strike the income statement are reasonably straight forward once one has a mastery of the seeming reversal caused by the tax consequences. The rather odd results that these entries may have argues that, from the point of view of managerial accounting, they should be kept separate and neither lumped in with other income or expense accounts nor netted, or they will give some misleading information as to the success of operations.

Bookkeeping Accounts Which May Be Useful

Titles	Purpose
Asset accounts	
Cash:	Payment of insurance premium. Receipt of proceeds at death. Payments to employee-survivors.
Prepaid premiums:	Put expense into appropriate period.
Surrender value, dividend accumulation:	Record predeath policy values.
Liability accounts	
Deferred Compensation contract payable:	Accrue present value of obligations.
Allowance for income taxes:	Reflect tax credit on payments.
Income accounts	
Increase in policy values:	Show periodic growth in pre-death policy.
Proceeds of life-insurance policy:	Receipt of cash at death.
Expense	
Gross premium:	Payments to insurance company.
Deferred Compensation payments:	Payments to participants.
Deferred Compensation:	Accrue liability during working period.

Journal Entries

This entry (A) is to record transaction in a nondeath year where the liability to the participant is a remote contingency and is addressed in the financials only as a footnote. The premium is $4,393 in this example, and the net surrender value increases by $5,240.

Entry A

	Asset— Cash		Expense— Gross premium	
	DR	CR	DR	CR
Payment of premium:		$4,393	$4,393	

	Asset— Surrender Value		Income— Increase in Value	
	DR	CR	DR	CR
Increase in surplus:	$5,240			$5,240

Thus the transactions for the year:

Income	$5,240
Expense	$4,393
Net	$ 847

There are several cautions that need to be observed:

1. The expense is not a tax deductible item.
2. The expense may be an allowable item on certain type of cost-plus and similar contracts. If so it should not be netted against the buildup of surplus and it will be advisable to use the entry procedures as shown in B and accrue the liability.
3. The income and asset buildup are not taxable.
4. Some authorities believe that the proper entry for the increase in cash value would be as a contra to the gross premium. This will, in most Deferred Compensation plans, develop into a negative expense in years after the first year.

This entry (B) is to record transactions in a nondeath year where the liability to the participant is to be accrued and is equal to the premium (using the same example as in A):

Entry B

	Asset— Cash		Expense— Gross premium	
	DR	CR	DR	CR
Payment of premium:		$4,393	$4,393	

	Asset— Surrender Value		Income— Increase in Value	
	DR	CR	DR	CR
Increase in surplus:	$5,240			$5,240

	Liability— Deferred Compensation		Expense— Deferred Compensation	
	DR	CR	DR	CR
Obligation to participants::		$4,393	$4,393	

Note again the tax issues and notes pertaining to A.

This entry (C) is to record receipt of proceeds at death: for example, receiving $400,000 where the surrender value had been $58,321. Note that the income is not taxable.

Entry C

	Asset— Cash		Income— Proceeds of life insurance	
	DR	CR	DR	CR
Receipt of the cash and: offset-surrender value:	$400,000			$341,679

	Asset— Surrender Value	
	DR	CR
		$58,321

It should be noted that this income is not taxable.

This entry (D) is to record payment to the employee or beneficiary where the liability has not been accrued in a prior period: for example, the payment is $20,000, the firm's expected tax rate 30 percent. (These payments may be subject to withholding tax but should be immune from FICA, FUDA, etcetera, if agreement is properly drawn.)

Entry D

	Asset— Cash		Expense— Deferred Compensation	
	DR	CR	DR	CR
Making the payment:		$20,000	$20,000	

	Liability— Allow for Tax		Expense— Tax Payable	
	DR	CR	DR	CR
Accruing the tax advantage and reducing tax payable:	$6,000			$6,000

Income	$ 0
Expense	$20,000
Expense	($ 6,000) reduction in tax expense
Net	$14,000

This entry (E) is to record payment to employee or beneficiary where the liability has been accrued in a prior period and uses the same figures as in D. (The previously expensed accrual of the obligation which was not a tax deductible expense when accrued has now become deductible. Consequently there is an expense deduction and no expense.)

Entry E

	Asset— Cash		Liability— Deferred Compensation	
	DR	CR	DR	CR
Making the payment:		$20,000		$20,000

	Liability— Allowance for Tax		Expense— Tax Payable	
	DR	CR	DR	CR
Accruing the tax:	$6,000			$6,000

Income	$ 0
Expense	($6,000)
Net	($6,000)

Cash Flow

A common question encountered when designing a Deferred Compensation plan is what will be the effect on the cash flow. What is really being asked is how rigid are premium-deposit requirements. Unlike qualified plans where the IRS requires a justification for missing payments, mortality-funded Deferred Compensation freely permits stop-start funding when the firm has a reason (or no reason) to postpone the annual premium deposit. The technique, which financial planners call minimum depositing, involves borrowing a portion of the policy cash value to pay the current year's premium. Payment of the current year's premium creates an increase in the cash value which will allow for further borrowing in the subsequent year. The policy loans create an interest obligation, typically at a very favorable rate such as 8 percent on the traditional whole-life contract. This may vary on those contracts in which the equity portion is designed to respond to current interest rates. The interest is a deductible expense to the firm if it has paid or will pay in full the premium for four of the first seven years of the policy. Using minimum deposit the firm could go on for many years with no cash being put into the preretirement funding and still not jeopardize the mortality funding of the plan. The safety net is, of course, being eroded, and it is important not to lose sight of the objective of having the policy fully paid up and the safety net in place by the time the employee reaches retirement.

The basic idea of mortality-funded Deferred Compensation is that postretirement payments to participants will be paid from the firm's operations, and the policy and the safety net will sit dormant on the balance sheet until a death precipitates the tax-free inflow of cash. As a practical matter the firm may wish to eat away at the surplus in such a way as to zero out its cash flow. Here again the appropriate technique would be to use minimum deposit. It is even possible to borrow out the entire cash value. This seems an anomaly since all life-insurance contracts offer the built-in opportunity to surrender the policy for an annuity based on the cash value. However, it is axiomatic that the life-insurance policy is only cancelled or surrendered as a last resort since that move instantly defeats the inherent tax leverage that allows the proceeds to be received tax free. Minimum depositing during the retirement years can be very attractive since the annual increase in the cash value of the paid-up policy may be greater than the net after-tax cost of borrowing from the policy at the low contract rate.

A further use of minimum deposit would be to preserve an optionally higher death benefit. It is often wise to design the plan so that in addition to its being paid up at the time of the employees retirement the opportunity exists to continue payments and have a much higher death benefit. If at that time the employee is in a state of health that suggests that electing the higher death benefit is the wiser course, this can be done without incurring an adverse cash flow by using minimum deposit.

Notes

1. American Institute of Certified Public Accountants handbook, *AICPA Professional Standards,* as of June 1980, section 4064.01.

2. Ibid., section 4063.157.

3. Quoted from ERISA. For further discussion, see appendix C.

4. *AICPA Professional Standards,* section 4064.01.

11 Caveats and Cautions

The Unsecured Promise to Pay

The funding of a Deferred Compensation plan is necessarily an unrestricted asset of the firm, and the employee may have no secured interest in the funds. Professional advisors concerned with long-term planning for retirement are sometimes preconditioned by their exposure to qualified plans in which the funding is unassailable by the firm's creditors. As a result they become alarmed about this vulnerability of Deferred Compensation's funding. The owner of the business, whose investment in the business is always at risk, often sees this in just the opposite light: the creation of additional internal reserves and the gaining and keeping of key people may be the major ingredient in the success, and even survival, of the firm, and, consequently, the ability of the owner to create a retirement plan for himself and his employees. Nevertheless, the possibility always exists that the firm could become so inextricably involved in problems that it could not continue to operate, and other creditors would be able to invade the funding that has been generated for the Deferred Compensation plan.

Timely recognition of the problem will assist in developing a strategy that is the least damaging. One worst-case possibility is that of giving up the title to the individual life-insurance policies, and any side-funding vehicle, to the participants or switching their interest in the funding to a secured one. This must, of course, be done sufficiently in advance of a bankruptcy to avoid giving a preference to the participants over other creditors. It also makes the receipt by the participants a taxable event for them. Another more attractive option would be a sale of the firm, or a portion thereof, in such a way that it would be a package including the Deferred Compensation contracts of the participants and the associated funding. Given that the assumptions as to earnings, interest, and tax leverage would be valid for the purchaser too, the sale could salvage the plan and be profitable for the purchaser as well.

It is the general nature of Deferred Compensation plans that they are for the benefit of the insiders who will be in a position to recognize problems that impact the plan in the same way that their owner's equity would be impacted and take appropriate action. Of course, they must be properly apprised of the situation.

Postretirement Security

As with the unsecured promise to pay, it is possible to foresee some situations where some uncertainty develops as to the long-range ability of the firm to perform under its agreement. For example, an owner-participant who, through retirement and/or the sale of the firm, becomes divorced from the day-to-day activities might develop such a concern. There are a number of guarantees that might be introduced to address this concern. The particular circumstances of the firm will dictate how best to proceed, and, since this is a very fine line, it should obviously be handled with the assistance of tax-knowledgeable counsel. Avenues that could be explored would include the kinds of generalized credit assurances that any large unsecured creditor might demand:

1. Personal endorsement of the principals, or
2. Continuing warranties as to the financial condition of the firm, for example, the net worth would not be allowed to drop below a certain point, the working capital to be maintained at a ratio above a certain point, prohibitions against mortgaging or sale of major assets, dilution, or dimunition of ownership.

Although the participants may not gain a secured position without suffering a tax disadvantage, there is no reason why a position worse than any of the general creditors is required. Thus, it may be posited that *continuing* to extend credit to a faltering firm is not required. Some indices as to required creditworthiness might be used as triggers to end the participant's creditor relationship for the long contractual obligation as a retired participant. At the very least it is recommended that some provision such as that given in the sample Deferred Compensation agreement which deals with merger, consolidation, or other take over of the firm be utilized (paragraph fifteen, change of business form of appendix H).

Trusts and Escrow Accounts

As has been repeatedly pointed out, the Deferred Compensation plan must be *unfunded* in the IRS meaning of that word in order for participants to avoid current taxation. An early temptation of concerned drafters is to find a way in which to capture and isolate funds for an individual participant. Unfortunately, this seems always to run afoul of IRC Section 83(c): Reg. 1.83 0 3(c) dealing with constructive receipt. The theory of constructive receipt is that a person cannot turn his back for tax purposes on income he has a right to receive. In Deferred Compensation an employee will have been found to have gained constructive receipt and the *economic benefit* of the funding at the earliest time that his benefit is either transferable or not subject to substantial risk of forfeiture.

Most of the efforts to escape seem to center on introducing a *risk* of forfeiture. It is the IRS's view that such a risk must be substantial, so the use of a risk that might only be regarded as nominal may be self-defeating. Where the effort to use a trust or escrow account, or to otherwise isolate the funds, is applicable to postretirement period, the problem intensifies. A covenant not to compete, for example, which might be considered *substantive* for an employee age fifty, may be considered less so when he reaches age sixty-five. Suffice it to say that the intent of the law is unambiguous, and avoiding the letter of it should be done with great caution.

Split Dollar

Some authorities have advocated a separation of the preretirement death benefit from the retirement and postretirement death benefit. The argument for this is that it allows the proceeds to go directly to the employee's beneficiary without income tax. The use of the split-dollar method in which the employee pays for the mortality portion of the policy (usually offset with a bonus) and the firm pays for the equity portion accomplishes this objective. Although Deferred Compensation is too flexible to make hard and fast rules about what will always work best, this book leans away from this technique. In using the split dollar the employee is taxed during his working life for the economic benefit of the protection he is afforded, but this may be only a modest disadvantage. More important is the fact that the employer would lose both the pay-out deductibility of the payments to the employee's family and the discounted value of those payments which would typically be spread over ten or fifteen years. These two elements, and the fact that the proceeds at death go directly to the bottom line of the firm without tax, are key elements in the mortality-funding concept. The decision no doubt rests on where the greatest leverage can be obtained considering the tax position of the employee's survivors and that of the firm.

Minimum Deposit

The stop-start flexibility of mortality-funded Deferred Compensation uses the borrowing out of some of the funds to sustain the plan when cash flow is low or for other reasons. This ironing out of the unevenness in the firm's funds flow has been pointed out as providing a further tax leverage because the borrowing of surplus from one's own life-insurance policies creates an interest obligation that is of itself tax deductible. Practitioners will recognize that payment in full of interest rather than offsetting provides a greater certainty of the deduction. It should also be remembered that the IRS requires that a minimum of four of the first seven years of premium payment must be made in full, or a legitimate business reason exist for the loan, in order to avail oneself of this tax deduction.

ERISA

Although Deferred Compensation plans are immune from the tedious rules of ERISA and IRS-qualified plans, there is an obligation for those firms who would fall under ERISA rules to register the existence of the plan. The requirements for immunity are that the plan be for a select group of management or highly compensated employees and that the benefits be funded by insurance policies or the general assets of the firm. A statement to that effect should be filed with the secretary of labor.

Social Security

The appendix dealing with resolutions and agreements treats the issue of how best to lessen the contributions that employees must make to FICA and the matching contributions by their employers. The general purpose is to avoid such obligations after retirement. This requires that the firm establish a *plan* for a class or classes of employees (even if there is but one employee) separately from the Deferred Compensation agreement which, in turn, is separate from the employment contract of the employee. In the past the employees have, typically, been above the FICA threshold so the preretirement exposure to contributions was moot. As Social Security extends its grasp upwards to the more highly paid, it will be necessary to watch so that participants are not unnecessarily taxed nor inadvertently deprived of future Social Security benefits.

The Terminating Employee

The employer will have the best insight into how an employee should be treated who is terminated. The almost inexhaustible options inherent in Deferred Compensation will allow the plan designer to meet any requirement the employer may desire. The ingredients that influence the decision are the proximity to ownership, the perception of the employee as a possible competitive threat, and the employer's posture that the plan essentially represents a reward for services already performed. Thus, quite different treatments will need to be devised for the founder, president, major-stockholder employee, and the world-class-marketing-vice-president employee who has just been hired away from a competitor.

For the employee who might become a competitor the golden handcuffs theory would be exploited as far as the negotiations with the employee would allow. A huge benefit with a huge forfeiture provision meets this need. In any event, the right to any quick cash (such as the commuted value of the benefits earned to a certain point or the cash value of the policy being used to fund the benefits) should be denied as it might form the platform for launching a competitor.

For the owner-founder employee it is obvious that the plan cannot be designed to squeeze him out of any benefits. However, it may be politically attractive to include some forfeiture provisions similar to those that are being imposed on other employees. This not only gives a feeling of fairness among the participants but placates second-echelon employees who could be concerned that the strong effective leader in whose wake they are finding success might be attracted away.

Where the participants are included in the plan for past services as a paternalistic supplement to any other retirement benefits, it would not be uncommon for the employer to take a no-gain, no-loss posture. This would entail allowing the employee the value of whatever funding was in place at the time of termination. Options could include cash, an immediate but reduced stream of payments, or a stream of benefits to start at the death or normal retirement date (adjusted for the fact that the employee terminated early).

Some of the flexibility in working out these arrangements stems from the use of mortality funding through life insurance. Different from other forms of insurance, the life-insurance policy requires no *insurable interest* when it matures at death. That is, the employer holding a policy on the life of an ex-employee need not show that he suffers any loss when the employee dies, but he may still collect the face value of the policy. This opens up various options, such as continuing to keep the policy in full force even though the reason for which it was initiated is gone, accepting a paid-up policy in a reduced amount that will some day pay off and in which the cash values are still accessible to the employer, or terminating the policy for its surrender value. It is also possible to sell the policy to the employee, his subsequent employer, or anyone else. The price could be the net surrender value, in which case the buyer would have sufficient funds in the policy to make the payment or some other amount. The governing factors would be the beneficence of the employer, the size of the funds involved, the health of the employee, and the tax posture of all parties.

Anticipation of the consequences of the termination of any of the participants will permit the plan to be designed to meet that situation correctly.

Nothing prevents an employer from establishing a plan with provisions that assure the firm all the safety it needs with a view to the future possibility of individually and selectively liberalizing the rules as, and if, that becomes appropriate.

Suicide

Insurance policies have a provision that denies payment for deaths due to suicide during the first two years of the policy. For this reason it is recommended that any plan which gives substantial preretirement death benefits be designed to exclude suicide during that period.

Cross-Pooling

The traditional approach to Deferred Compensation took a more one-policy, one-employee view than does the funding with mortality approach. Funding with mortality, particularly where more than one employee is in the plan, borrows from the group-pension methodology seen in Deposit Administration and Immediate Participation Guarantee plans. In those plans actuarial assumptions are employed where sex, turnover, mortality, interest earnings, and benefits are factored to produce an undivided obligation of the employer. The obligation is then smoothed into regular payments that will meet the obligation. Further attention is addressed to the *emerging liability,* or those points at which plan participants begin to receive retirement benefits, to make certain that the smoothed payment funding will be sufficient to meet those individual obligations.

Legally, the traditional approach to Deferred Compensation gave no employee any more interest in *his* policy than any other employee because it was simply one of the undivided assets of the firm. Since the funding-with-mortality approach uses cross-pooling rather more straightforwardly, it may be useful for the participants to see that this entity concept not only allows for much larger benefits, but that it strengthens the plan for all concerned. If it can be seen that the ultimate undivided obligation of the employer is to be met by policies which are paid for during the working life of the employee, and that the safety net responds to the problem of emerging liability, the employees may be comforted to realize that their certainty of getting benefits is reinforced by the policy cash values and death proceeds of policies on the other participants.

As with group plans where an annual actuarial analysis is done annually, mortality-funded Deferred Compensation needs a similar, albeit less formal review. A carefully monitored Deferred Compensation plan is probably no more vulnerable to collapse, or wide-ranging cost fluctuations that might endanger it, than is the group plan. The analogy should not be pushed too far. Quite different tax forces are at work. Group plans gain no advantage from a death apart from a reduced liability, and consequently more often than not do not provide benefits to survivors for preretirement deaths. The differences can be thought of as subtractive for the group plan and additive for the Deferred Compensation plan.

Underfunding

A certified financial statement following standard rules for auditing would show that the firm has a Deferred Compensation plan which creates an obligation, although it may only be a contingent obligation. It would similarly show that the downstream liability was being accrued for in the current period. This appears to be no problem where the safety net is being developed. The rules also recognize that, where the obligation is remote either in possibility or in time, a deferral in establishing a safety net would not be a barrier to giving an *unqualified* audit. In the extreme case, such as the promise to pay a twenty-one-year-old employee a retirement benefit at age sixty-five if he remains with the firm until that time, it is quite clear that developing a surplus to meet that obligation is not immediately necessary. However, if the employer is entering into Deferred Compensation agreements with some employees and planning in the near term on funding those obligations with term insurance that only covers the preretirement death obligation (as is not uncommon for middle management and younger employees), it may be wise to check that the auditors will not take exception. In general, the addition of participants at younger ages, protected with term insurance, can be demonstrated as enhancing the plan. A preretirement death, the probability of which can be calculated, will produce a funds flow greater than the immediate obligation, thus stabilizing the plan for the remaining participants. In a particular situation it may be easiest to tighten up the vesting so as to increase the possibility of a forfeiture by the employee. This pushes the obligation into a more remote position and should permit deferring the safety net.

The Uninsurable Individual

Uninsurability poses a complexity in pulling together a Deferred Compensation plan. Given the current state of the market, the first question that should be addressed is: is this a truly uninsurable person? The capacity of the industry to cope with very seriously impaired health situations has expanded enormously in the past decade. Some experts in the field of substandard placements would doubt that a person working full time could properly be described as uninsurable. It may be that turning to such an expert to seek offers before patching the plan together in some other way is the first remedy.

The last resort of the impaired risk specialists is usually some form of scale-up life-insurance plan. In this the death benefits start small, or simply involves in the early periods, a return of premium and then progressively grows to reasonable limits. This indeed compares rather poorly with a standard life-insurance contract but because the prime objective of a Deferred Compensation plan is to have a fully paid-up life-insurance contract in place by the time of retirement, it may be an acceptable substitute. The reason being that, if it will have grown to a sufficiently high mortality value at retirement age, the tax leverage (being received income-tax free and ultimately providing the funds to balance tax-deductible payments to the recipient) continues to be valid. The fairness of the extra charge for the worsened mortality is another issue quite beyond the scope of this text. Suffice it to say that the best test is that of the market. If the risk has had a fair exposure to the highly competitive substandard marketplace, the plan designer can feel that the loading built into the best offer is closely tuned to the real projected mortality of the risk. The predictability of an inflow of funds, using the probability of the CSO table, is lost. Appendix A includes a way in which the loading can be used to deduce and quantify the higher expected mortality. As a practical matter it may be sufficient to recognize that it is a higher probability.

Totally uninsurable participants, or those for whom only scale-up policies can be obtained, may need the death-before-retirement aspect of their individual Deferred Compensation contracts reworked to fit the scale-up. Not uncommonly, a participant will have erected a mental defense against accepting the consequences implicit in his or her medical history. This manifests itself in an unwillingness to accept a less than standard policy (no matter how mild the surcharge), an unwillingness to cooperate to obtain competitive bids of carriers dealing in the area of special health problems, and often complete rejection of the importance of the predeath benefit and mortality funding. The result may be the striking out in the direction of installment-purchase-deferred annuities or simply the creation of a sinking fund through some investment vehicle. The disadvantges are substantial.

The human problem of dealing honestly and fairly with the impaired risk is also beyond the scope of this text. It may be necessary in some cases to fit in an annuity or side fund to accommodate the personalities involved. A better solution, where there are more participants than just the one having a health problem, is to readdress the plan as an entity by bumping the death-benefit amounts on other participants and also raising the safety net to offset the fact that, for one particular participant, there will be zero mortality-funds inflow. A quite acceptable and understandable plan can usually be developed. The preretirement death remains a problem. However, it may be possible to temporize by using an unrelated, completely nonmedical program of group insurance structured to favor that individual. Sometimes this type of program has several layers, and the sum of them can reach a quite respectable limit. This is practical if the firm has a sufficiently large number of employees to provide an underwriting base.

Annuities, Side Funds, Sinking Funds, and Investments

The traditional approach to Deferred Compensation pushed the life-insurance-policy-cash or surrender values as the resource from which benefits at retirement were to be drawn. The death aspect got major attention only as it dealt with the problem of preretirement deaths. As such, and to the degree that plan designers continue to use that approach, the life-insurance vehicle becomes a fair target for competition from other media where the yield may be projected to be, or actually be, higher. While the life-insurance industry scrambles to adjust its front-end pricing to real-time interest rates with products such as Universal Life, Current Assumption Life, new money concepts and other schemes (all of which, by the way, will be suitable for use in the Deferred Compensation plan), it has ignored its primary area of expertise—dealing with mortality. A rather less well advertised area of expertise, that of legislative lobbying for favorable tax treatment, is also ignored.

Deferred Compensation plans funded with mortality can easily weather the bulge in interest rates even using traditional whole-life products. The interest bulge, over a period of time, will be squeezed back to the consumer in dividends and/or lower front-end costs as new participants are added. The most important ingredient is the use of the leverage of mortality. If, for reasons of health for example, it becomes necessary to use a vehicle where the proceeds are unsheltered, the fund accumulation, of necessity, will be much larger. Said another way, the safety net will need to be greatly enriched. A range of 30 percent to 60 percent of the ultimate obligation will usually be sufficient for a mortality-funded safety net, but it will be obvious that a safety net for a pure sinking fund will need to approach 100 percent. Annuities in which the interest accumulation of the funds is untaxed until taken may be the best avenue when life insurance is totally unavailable.

12 Some Thoughts for Practitioners

The satisfaction derived from having designed, established, and gotten running a sound Deferred Compensation plan is enormous. However, just as in the case of an architect, the opportunity to use hard-won skills and see the product of them reach fruition, depends upon finding and persuading a client to undertake the project. Perhaps, therefore, it is not inappropriate for a book that attempts to bring together a general understanding of all of the aspects of a Deferred Compensation plan to also address this important professional skill as well.

The Prospects

The broad range of organizations that can and do profit from Deferred Compensation makes any narrow definition of the *best* prospects next to impossible. Indeed the selection of the type of businesses to approach is truly a subjective one—more a matter of personality and interest than known predilection for needing Deferred Compensation. Perhaps it would be wise, at least in the beginning, to work with small, closely held firms. Small might mean firms with fewer than one hundred employees, or maybe small in the sense that the controlling ownership is held by the owners, who number three or four, and who are active in the day-to-day running of the firm. Larger firms become targets for the prestige specialist. Size drift-up can be expected as the array of successful cases grows and the professional community begins to recognize experience and proficiency.

Small firms have a number of advantages: where the logical participants are the owner/operators, the building of internal surplus adds materially to their day-to-day job security. The relationships in small firms are often sorted out in a way that makes decisions easier and plan design less vulnerable to the convolutions of the pecking order prevalent in larger firms. The complexities of ERISA, and the inelasticity of qualified plans weigh heavily on small firms—nearly to the point of harassment. Smallness of size brings no essential diminution in the compliance and paperwork burdens associated with governmental intervention. Again, like the architects, the practioner's compensation tracks with the size of the project. Two or three Deferred Compensation cases, which is the case load a practioner might be able to add onto his existing annual activities, could average

$15,000 to $30,000 in premium each. This is a respectable addition and very likely easier than one large case.

The conventional wisdom might lead away from situations where the prospective participants are at ages near retirement, or there is a suspicion of a health issue that would make finding a market for life insurance difficult. There are ways to work out most of these problems, and their existence frequently adds motivation, both to the prospective participant with this condition and those who are his colleagues. On balance it does not seem wise to circumvent an otherwise accessible and qualified prospect.

Existing clients are the currency that keeps all professionals busy. In financial planning this is equally true. Deferred Compensation forms a good fit with items like pension plans, profit-sharing plans, and group insurance. Prior key-person-life-insurance sales, and Section 79 cases (particularly where it was a term-life carve-out to bring coverage on a few employees to a high limit) are clear signals that Deferred Compensation should be considered.

It is axiomatic in selling that a suspect is not a prospect unless he has the financial ability to buy. This is, of course, true in Deferred Compensation also. However, if the test is too stringently applied good prospects may be overlooked. A firm may not have demonstrated any ability to build reserves or produce consistent bottomline profits and still find the wherewithal to launch a successful Deferred Compensation plan if its leaders are motivated to do so. Small firms have ways and reasons to manipulate their earnings to strip out profits. Service businesses or other businesses not capital intensive are particularly inclined to do that. Developing surplus for a firm is somewhat like accumulating savings in that it requires discipline and planning. For all the concern and discussion about gaining a point or two of higher yield—with this or that investment—most searchers for wealth are thwarted by their failure to build the savings to which yield might apply. It is one of the obscure virtues of whole-life-insurance products that they force savings. It may also be a useful corollary of a Deferred Compensation plan that it enforces the accumulation of surplus.

Motivation

In seeking to gain decisions it is not enough to have an irrefutable logical program that fits together like a jigsaw puzzle. The decision will be made on the basis of the perception of how well the program responds to the needs of whoever is making the decision. The professional who wishes to sell his program should be clear about what needs he is addressing in order to be effective. The work of Abraham Maslow is useful in this respect.[1] Maslow developed a hierarchy of human needs and established that humans were unable to transition up the scale to the more sophisticated needs until each of the more fundamental needs was met. The sequence, starting at the bottom is *physical needs* (food, water); *need for safety; social needs* (or love); *the need for esteem* (prestige or recognition); *the need for self-respect* (confirmation of one's value); and *the need for self-actualization* (developing one's talents).

Using Maslow's ideas it becomes necessary to sell up the line using the lowest ranking needs that are appropriate. If Maslow is right this is true not simply because they are strongest, but because leaping over an unsatisfied need to a higher ranked one provides no motivation at all. It is not demeaning to be addressing fundamental needs, quite apart from the fact that they are the most powerful motivators. Fundamental needs are common to everyone and only by having satisfied them can one go on to higher levels of human achievement.

Deferred Compensation is certainly not a panacea for all needs, but it responds strongly to the three lowest rungs on the ladder very well. It is easy to relate the existence of a standing surplus to food and water. It is equally easy to translate the future stream of income into an insulation or safety, and the needs for social intercourse and love are recognized in the gift of security beyond the ability to provide it during life. In simpler terms Maslow points out an unalterable need to look out for one's own self.

Selling Deferred Compensation as an intentionally discriminatory plan has a mild shock value. It may be particularly useful in that it shifts the advocacy of this slightly asocial posture to the professional. The need, of course, lies with the listener and is a very strong motivation. The ability to address this need runs into conflict with some other signals. Employers, particularly in the United States and more particularly small employers, have a paternalistic role toward their employees. They feel the responsibility for their health, welfare, success and prosperity, and they most often feel that they are generous, fair, and equitable toward their employees and that it is these characteristics that have allowed them to build a productive organization. Some of the conditioning arises from the laws and tax postures of the government, but a good deal arises out of the concept of democracy as a social system rather than only a method of government. The manifestations of this altruism are uniform rules and benefits for everyone or everyone by class: identical medical care, uniform working hours, standard vacation allowances, one common lunch room, and so forth. The employer may at the same time experience no problem with enjoying a salary that reflects his greater experience and knowledge and risk and responsibility burdens. The effect of this dichotomy is often a reverse discrimination in which the economic effort of the firm for nonsalaried benefits is proportionately less for the top people than for the average. Using Deferred Compensation to reverse this reverse discrimination is a powerful motivational tool.

Another sequencing of needs is chronological. This concept postulates that needs evolve as a function of age. One starts with fun and pleasure, makes the transition through success, recognition, and prestige, and finally reaches the need to be memorialized. Deferred Compensation decision makers are often at the far end of this line. The plan responds by adding a measure of certainty that the firm will survive and be perpetuated. This has a substantial significance when there are following generations and should not be underestimated in any case. A firm that represents the life work of an individual may be more important to him by far than the value of the bricks, mortar, and good will.

A final motivational concept of value is that of the herd instinct. It is an established fact that decisions that are taken collectively are bolder than those taken individually. This may not argue for trying to find a committee to whom a Deferred Compensation plan can be sold, but it does argue for giving the decision maker the comfort of knowing that other wise and successful people have reached the same decision. The answer may be no more complicated than saying that 90 percent of the New York Stock Exchange members had some form of Deferred Compensation or the citing of particular firms known to have such plans. The art of managerial decision making involves extrapolating from insufficient data enough information to make decisions. Breaking new ground would require a step-up in the amount of data needed. The existence of plans reinforces a bent towards a positive decision and acts as a comfort factor in the postdecision ambivalence.

Presentations

Given that the decision makers will not seek an exhaustive knowledge of the issue and have but a limited time to gain an understanding a very simple summary of the highlights is useful to capture interest. The primary focus should be on the benefits, leaving the cost and techniques a lesser role. Aim high. Use an income of at least 50 percent of the participants' current incomes. This may appear to be a big number, particularly when other sources are known to exist, but it makes the project worth considering. The often-quoted Parkinson's Law that "expenditure rises to meet income" is a serious reality. People with even very large incomes often have a matching life style, nothing left over, and no comfortable view of how they would cope with a future reduction in income.

There are certain ideas that need to be conveyed to the prospect. There seems to be a fascination with mortality and the cumulative probability of at least one death. Since that idea is central to funding Deferred Compensation with mortality, it is pleasant to find how quickly and easily it is understood. That discussion leads itself naturally into the tax ramifications. It seems unnecessary to be immodest about the long-term success of the lobbying efforts of the life-insurance industry. The tax-free receipt of the policy proceeds at death and the deductibility of the payments to participants are important features of the plan. It is an aspect of the social-engineering part of the tax laws that they encourage the purchase of life insurance, both to lessen the society's problems with indigent widows and orphans and as a capital formation vehicle. It behooves anyone who is able to do so to take advantage of these laws.

Preconditioning to the idea that all expenses of the firm should be designed to be deductible often brings a moment's pause. It is usually very easy to convince anyone relative to (a) tax immunity for the proceeds and no deductibility for the premiums or (b) taxability of the proceeds and deductibility of the premiums—that the life-insurance lobby won the battle. But the extra leverage for choice (a) in Deferred Compensation should be stressed. The safety net of Deferred Compensation is accumulated internally and after the first year the premium payment is essentially a transfer between two surplus accounts (cash and the surrender or cash value of the life insurance policies) so that the tax deductibility of the premiums becomes moot. The undeductible premium situation quickly reverses so that the in-flow of cash value is greater than the premium, and this fortunately is not taxed as income (another lobbying battle won).

The internalized surplus accumulation is very important to the audience to whom the professional speaks. It goes directly to the lower rungs of Maslow's hierarchical ladder and should of course be emphasized. An anomaly is created by the growth of surplus which balances out the expense of premiums, giving the sensation that the plan costs nothing. The cost, of course, is real and should be explained as such. It is also important to point out that the plan assets, while available for opportunities and emergencies, are consequently vulnerable to the claims of other creditors. The techniques and limitations of defending against such claims should be explored. Above all, be candid and professional and do not skirt what might be regarded as bad news. A brief summary of other retirement-funding vehicles and their advantages may be in order.

The net present value concept may be as familiar to the prospect as to his advisors. If not, the idea needs to be explained and understood. The mystery of doing the mathematics can be ignored. Even for business people who understand net present value, the idea of lifetime income being worth less than an income for fifteen years may need some support. A firm price for a single-premium annuity at age sixty-five is usually satisfactory and can be put into the full proposal together with the individual and consolidated ledger analysis for all the contracts that are being proposed.

Listening and Asking

After weeks of preparation of a carefully manicured proposal or even at the fact-finding interview, the temptation to lecture and pronounce may be as understandable as it is inexcusable. The great flexibility of Deferred Compensation lends itself to solving many issues, and the cookie-cutter approach that worked in one case may be totally unsuitable for another. The only way to find out what is needed is to ask and listen—another parallel with the architect whose stock in trade is to be able to customize the project to any needs, sites, budgets, etcetera. Just as with the architect, the retirement planner needs a great deal of input: ages, salaries, key employees, tax postures, interest assumptions, perpetuation plans, and the like. It may even be wise to prepare a set of questions to be asked as a starting point. It is seldom unflattering to solicit opinions, and the information can be key to the success of the plan. It is also not unflattering to sit and take notes from the statements that are being made. Each case might need a different set of questions or similar questions in different form:

> What is your view of interest trends over the longer term, say, fifteen years?

> Do you foresee your firm continuing to have about the same corporate income-tax rate in the foreseeable future?

> What concerns you most about your business?

> As and when you retire, will the firm continue pretty much as is?

> Is the sale of this type of business easy to arrange?

> Who are the people in your organization that you really need to tie in?

> Has it been your pattern to accumulate surpluses? Would that be desirable?

> Do you have or do your partners have family who might come into the business? and so on.

Interfacing with Other Professionals

Having a good attorney to draft the agreement is an essential. The manner in which the plan designer interfaces with the attorney (and perhaps the accountant) is critical to the success of the plan. Sometimes professional financial planners believe that their plans are unwarrantedly thwarted by other professionals, but this implies a failure to work the intraprofessional relationships correctly. The general relationship will be dictated by the client. A large portion, perhaps the majority of executives, are good decision makers who only need and want factual input and intelligent execution by their professional advisors. They believe that business decisions are best made by business people and that advisors only add parameters within their area of expertise. Another group employs its advisors as a part of the management team where their breadth of experience and professional training add a dimension to the decision mix.

Whatever the pattern established by the client, it is important to work up a professional-to-professional communication. Consider the attorney's position. He has as much of a need to convince the client of his value as does the plan designer. It would be a very rare attorney who had spent as much time and study of Deferred Compensation or the particular plan under examination by the client as the plan designer will have. When uncertainty clouds the decision, the human reaction is to slow down. The answer is to remove the uncertainty. The plan designer should share resource material. These could include material from R. & R. Newkirk, selections from Prentice Hall's sample agreements, or tax and legal-service information from Commercial Clearing House, as well as insurance-company samples and studies and generalized material such as this book or other texts which treat Deferred Compensation.

The material may, of course, be useful, but equally important is the intent of being a knowledgeable contributor and demonstrating that the area of expertise of the attorney is recognized and enhanced. Providing resources for the attorney builds rather than denigrates the attorney. It is certainly no secret to either the attorney or the client that insurance companies spend a great deal of money on highly skilled legal help in support of their marketing effort. That these efforts are self-serving in no way contaminates their validity. No right-thinking attorney would shun solid important research, nor would his client expect him to do so. None of the parties in solving the issues being treated by a Deferred Compensation plan—the client, the attorney, the legal researchers for the insurance companies, and most of all the plan designer—is interested in being involved with a flawed plan.

If good homework, sound thinking, research support, and good communications defuse potential problems and slow-downs by attorneys who work for the type of client who makes his own decisions and leaves his attorney the technician's role, a bit more is needed where the attorney or CPA is a part of the decision-making process. In such cases they legitimately need to be sold. This might involve the brief survey of other options: pensions, profit sharing, Keoghs, bonus plans, split dollar, family protection life insurance, sinking funds—and the reasons they were less suitable. The major barriers that are likely to be encountered center around the vulnerability of the funding to other creditors. This is an understandable and excusable reservation. It is likely that their experience has largely been with qualified, all-employee plans in which that is an important feature. It is also likely that, by-and-large, they are not entrepreneurs. That being so, their careers are not so intrinsically linked to a firm, they seldom have a capital investment to protect, nor have they experienced the vagaries and problems that plague business people in which the buttressing effect of additional surplus for real-time problems far outweighs the significance of a downstream danger. Again it is an educational problem, but in this instance the best support may be the client himself who does understand this trade-off.

An ancillary benefit of the good homework, good service, truly professional conduct, etcetera, is that this may be the ground for possible future relationship beneficial to both parties. The attorney may have other clients for whom a Deferred Compensation plan would be suitable, and the possibility of a recommendation exists. The other side of that coin is that there can hardly be a financial-planning person who has not been called upon to help find knowledgeable legal assistance. For pretty much these reasons some plan designers make a point of setting up meetings and seminars for attorneys and CPAs. As continuing education obligations grow for all professionals, it is safe to predict more of this cross-professional education will emerge and that it will inure to the benefit of all concerned.

The Current State of Life Insurance

The sales of ordinary life products skidded in inverse proportion to the soaring interest rates in the near-term past. A number of intertwined phenomena had an adverse effect: drain-out of funds in policy loans, inability to reinvest in long-term bonds being held at values way above the true market, punishment of new policyholders with old rates of return, flourishing of other competition for consumer investment dollars, rise in reinsurance availability, etcetera. Market changes are underway that will restore some of the balance.

Some part of the temporary discrediting of ordinary life arose from selling techniques that distorted the proper role of ordinary life insurance. These techniques focused on cash values, early cross-over points, quick cash-value accumulation, etcetera. Actuaries were urged onward to produce products for split dollar or minimum deposit that deemphasized the mortality aspect of the contract. The effect was to treat ordinary life products as cash-accumulation vehicles and to bring them into closer competition with the E.F. Huttons and the Merrill Lynches. With short-term interest rates popping through the roof, a no-win condition existed.

The public was not confused. It continued to see the function of life insurance as essential for its ability to deal with mortality. Any practitioner can testify that the face amounts of insurance have climbed far beyond his wildest expectations. The turn was not away from life insurance itself but to buying term and investing the difference. After measuring the cash-value growth against the money-market funds, the public rejected the pretense that ordinary life was an investment vehicle.

Funding Deferred Compensation with mortality and using up-to-date ordinary life products puts the issue back into the perspective in which it belongs. By using the tax leverage of mortality funding, the results defeat the incursions of E.F. Hutton and ends the unproductive contest in an area in which life-insurance companies had no place. The unquestioned necessity of completing the funding during the working life of the employee forestalls the buy-term-and-invest-the-difference strategy. The life-insurance professional has an important and valid niche here on which he might well wish to focus.

Service

As a final note it would be well to point out that the professional has not only an obligation, but an opportunity in the making of the periodic reviews of established cases. A number of issues may need to be addressed, and many of them would be additional business for him: revised estimates of interest or taxes that would call for a change in the safety net, raises, new employees, acquisitions, attracting new employees, etcetera. After the first year when the policy cash values begin to show up on the balance sheet at greater amounts than are being paid out in premiums, the firm gets a surge of confidence that the plan works. Sometimes this provokes an interest in extending the plan somewhat deeper into the ranks of employees.

Note

1. Abraham Maslow, *Motivation and Personality*, 2d ed. (New York: Harper & Row, 1970).

Appendix A
Commissioner's Standard Ordinary Mortality Table and Nonstandard Mortality

The Commissioner's Standard Ordinary Mortality Table (see table A-1) reflects the probability of the average insurable male. Obviously not everyone fits this category. In attempting to quantify the probability of a death in a small group or even an individual, it may be useful to have a somewhat more refined estimate.

Females have a longer life expectancy than males, and separate tables exist for female mortality. An acceptable way of allowing for this difference is the set-back method: use the same table but assume the female is three years younger. For example, in calculating the probability that a forty-seven-year-old female will reach sixty-five, use the probability that a forty-four-year-old male will reach sixty-two.

Substandard mortality may result from a variety of factors. Hazardous careers or avocational interests can be an influence. Perhaps more common among those for whom Deferred Compensation is of interest would be the health issues: blood pressure, weight, smoking, drinking, health history, family longevity, etcetera. One technique for getting some assessment of the impact of all of the factors is to deduce them from the judgment of life-insurance underwriters. The complex evaluation they make of all the interrelated variables comes in the end to percentage impact on standard mortality expectation. Using the results will provide a good index of worsened probability of death.

Particularly in the early policy years insurance companies enjoy a somewhat better experience with standard mortality than the CSO mortality table would predict and will for this reason and for competitive reasons use proprietary tables. This is primarily a result of the screening through which applicants are forced before they are offered a policy. Using a system of credits and debits, the applicant is assigned a numerical score relative to standard mortality. Scores differing from the mean by 20 percent or more above and 20-25 percent worse than standard are considered standard. A less favorable prediction of mortality is ranked in the order of severity. Either of two systems are used—the *class* system or the *table* system. They are the same and only differ semantically. The assignment of a substandard rating is not privileged information and is readily available from the company or agent. The table below translates the ratings into mortality.

Table A-1
1958 Commissioner's Standard Ordinary Mortality Table

Age	1 Number Living	2 Number Dying	3 Mortality Rate per 1,000	Expectation of Life	Age	4 Number Living	5 Number Dying	6 Mortality Rate per 1,000	Expectation of Life
0	10,000,000	70,800	7.08	68.04	50	8,762,306	72,902	8.32	23.23
1	9,929,200	17,475	1.76	67.34	51	8,689,404	79,160	9.11	22.43
2	9,911,725	15,066	1.52	66.45	52	8,610,244	85,758	9.96	21.64
3	9,896,659	14,449	1.46	65.55	53	8,524,486	92,832	10.89	20.86
4	9,882,210	13,835	1.40	64.64	54	8,431,654	100,337	11.90	20.10
5	9,868,375	13,322	1.35	63.73	55	8,331,317	108,307	13.00	19.34
6	9,855,053	12,812	1.30	62.81	56	8,223,010	116,849	14.21	18.60
7	9,842,241	12,401	1.26	61.89	57	8,106,161	125,970	15.54	17.88
8	9,829,840	12,091	1.23	60.97	58	7,980,191	135,663	17.00	17.16
9	9,817,749	11,879	1.21	60.04	59	7,844,528	145,830	18.59	16.47
10	9,805,870	11,865	1.21	59.12	60	7,698,698	156,592	20.34	15.78
11	9,794,005	12,047	1.23	58.19	61	7,542,106	167,736	22.24	15.12
12	9,781,958	12,325	1.26	57.26	62	7,374,370	179,271	24.31	14.46
13	9,769,633	12,896	1.32	56.33	63	7,195,174	191,174	26.57	13.83
14	9,756,737	13,562	1.39	55.41	64	7,003,925	203,394	29.04	13.21
15	9,743,175	14,225	1.46	54.49	65	6,800,531	215,917	31.75	12.61
16	9,728,950	14,983	1.54	53.57	66	6,584,614	228,749	34.74	12.02
17	9,713,967	15,737	1.62	52.65	67	6,355,865	241,777	38.04	11.46
18	9,698,230	16,390	1.69	51.74	68	6,114,088	254,835	41.68	10.91
19	9,681,840	16,846	1.74	50.83	69	5,859,253	267,241	45.61	10.39
20	9,664,994	17,300	1.79	49.92	70	5,592,012	278,426	49.79	9.88
21	9,647,694	17,655	1.83	49.00	71	5,313,586	287,731	54.15	9.39
22	9,630,039	17,912	1.86	48.09	72	5,025,855	294,766	58.65	8.93
23	9,612,127	18,167	1.89	47.18	73	4,731,089	299,289	63.26	8.47
24	9,593,960	18,324	1.91	46.27	74	4,431,800	301,894	68.12	8.03
25	9,575,636	18,481	1.93	45.36	75	4,129,906	303,011	73.37	7.60
26	9,557,155	18,732	1.96	44.45	76	3,826,895	303,014	79.18	7.19
27	9,538,423	18,981	1.99	43.54	77	3,523,881	301,997	85.70	6.79

Age	Number Living	Number Dying	Deaths per 1,000	Expectation of Life	Age	Number Living	Number Dying	Deaths per 1,000	Expectation of Life
28	9,519,442	19,324	2.03	42.62	78	3,221,884	299,829	93.06	6.41
29	9,500,118	19,760	2.08	41.71	79	2,922,055	295,683	101.19	6.04
30	9,480,358	20,193	2.13	40.80	80	2,626,372	288,848	109.98	5.69
31	9,460,165	20,718	2.19	39.88	81	2,337,524	278,983	119.35	5.36
32	9,439,447	21,239	2.25	38.97	82	2,058,541	265,902	129.17	5.05
33	9,418,208	21,850	2.32	38.06	83	1,792,639	249,858	139.38	4.76
34	9,396,358	22,551	2.40	37.15	84	1,542,781	231,433	150.01	4.47
35	9,373,807	23,528	2.51	36.24	85	1,311,348	211,311	161.14	4.20
36	9,350,279	24,685	2.64	35.33	86	1,100,037	190,108	172.82	3.94
37	9,325,594	26,112	2.80	34.42	87	909,929	168,455	185.13	3.69
38	9,299,482	27,991	3.01	33.52	88	741,474	146,997	198.25	3.44
39	9,271,491	30,132	3.25	32.63	89	594,477	126,303	212.46	3.20
40	9,241,359	32,622	3.53	31.74	90	468,174	106,809	228.14	2.96
41	9,208,737	35,362	3.84	30.85	91	361,365	88,813	245.77	2.72
42	9,173,375	38,253	4.17	29.97	92	272,552	72,480	265.93	2.47
43	9,135,122	41,382	4.53	29.10	93	200,072	57,881	289.30	2.22
44	9,093,740	44,741	4.92	28.24	94	142,191	45,026	316.66	1.96
45	9,048,999	48,412	5.35	27.38	95	97,165	34,128	351.24	1.69
46	9,000,587	52,473	5.83	26.53	96	63,037	25,250	400.56	1.39
47	8,948,114	56,910	6.36	25.69	97	37,787	18,456	488.42	1.06
48	8,891,204	61,794	6.95	24.86	98	19,331	12,916	668.15	.75
49	8,829,410	67,104	7.60	24.04	99	6,415	6,415	1,000.00	.50

Inasmuch as the rankings are obtained judgementally, they frequently vary from underwriter to underwriter and can be colored by the marketing strategy or proprietary mortality tables of the company. Still, they provide the best available prediction of worsened mortality.

An increased risk of dying at any given age naturally has a corresponding effect on the expected longevity of the individual. The approximate expectancy of newly insured males at various ages and in various classification is:

Age	Standard	Percentage			
		150	200	300	500
25	48	44	41	37	32
35	39	35	32	28	24
45	30	26	23	19	16
55	23	20	17	14	11
65	16	13	11	9	7

Thus a male age forty-five with a table D or class four substandard rating has a life expectancy of twenty-three years or seven years less than a standard forty-five-year old male (see table A-2).

Table A-2
Interpolating Substandard Mortality from Insurance Company Classification

Class	Table	Mortality Rate as Percentage of Standard
Standard	Standard	100
A	1	125
AA	1½	137
B	2	150
BB	2½	163
CC	3	175
D	4	200
E	5	225
F	6	250
G	7	275
H	8	300
I	9	325
J	10	350
K	11	375
L	12	400
M	13	425
N	14	450
O	15	475
P	16	500

The insurance company loads into its calculation only enough extra premium to balance the higher mortality. The dollar impact in any particular Deferred Compensation plan may be quite small. In any event the rationale for funding Deferred Compensation with mortality is not denigrated by a higher expectation of mortality—in fact it is reinforced.

Appendix B
Personal and
Corporate Federal
Income Tax Rates

Individual Income Tax Tables

Tax-Rate Schedules for Married Individuals Filing Joint Returns and Surviving Spouses

Taxable Income		1982 Pay	1982 Percentage on Excess[a]	1983 Pay	1983 Percentage on Excess[a]	1984 Pay	1984 Percentage on Excess[a]
$ 0	$ 3,400	0	0	0	0	0	0
3,400	5,500	0	12	0	11	0	11
5,500	7,600	$ 252	14	$ 231	13	$ 231	12
7,600	11,900	546	16	504	15	483	14
11,900	16,000	1,234	19	1,149	17	1,085	16
16,000	20,200	2,013	22	1,846	19	1,741	18
20,200	24,600	2,937	25	2,644	23	2,497	22
24,600	29,900	4,037	29	3,656	26	3,465	25
29,900	35,200	5,574	33	5,034	30	4,790	28
35,200	45,800	7,323	39	6,624	35	6,274	33
45,800	60,000	11,457	44	10,334	40	9,772	38
60,000	85,600	17,705	49	16,014	44	15,168	42
85,600	109,400	30,249	50	27,278	48	23,920	45
109,400	162,400	42,149	50	38,702	50	36,630	49
162,400	215,400	68,649	50	65,202	50	62,600	50
215,400		95,149	50	91,702	50	89,100	50

[a]The amount by which the taxpayer's taxable income exceeds the base of the bracket.

Corporate Income Tax Tables

Taxable Income Bracket Over	Taxable Income Bracket But Not Over	Tax Years Beginning in 1982	Tax Years Beginning in 1983
$ 0	$ 25,000	16%	15%
25,000	50,000	19	18
50,000	75,000	30	30
75,000	100,000	40	40
100,000	—	46	46

Appendix C
Resolutions and
Agreements: General
Legal Comments

These sample agreements and resolutions have been prepared as a guide to assist attorneys. They outline the basic provisions which are usually included in such agreements and resolutions. They are not intended as final drafts. Modifications may be required to fit the particular situation. The attorney will necessarily be responsible for the actual agreement or resolution and its wording.

General Comments

There are many different types of Deferred Compensation and salary-continuation agreements. Each agreement must be drafted by the attorney to meet the objectives of the parties and to fit the particular situation. The following pages provide sample resolutions, and a sample agreement with alternative provisions which may be appropriate for agreements between a closely held corporation and a key executive or stockholder-employee.

The sample agreement may be designed to fit a situation in which the agreement is employer motivated. The objective may be to help tie a key executive to the company, to attract a key executive from another company, or to supplement a qualified retirement plan. In these situations payment of the salary-continuation benefits will usually be conditional upon continuing employment with the company until retirement at a specified age, death, or disability. Other conditions such as not engaging in competition with the company after retirement or providing advisory or consulting services may be appropriate, and these are shown as alternative provisions. Such conditions are not necessary in order to prevent constructive receipt of income. The Internal Revenue Service has ruled that there will be no constructive receipt of income even though the employee's rights are nonforfeitable if (1) the agreement is entered into before the compensation is earned and (2) the employer's promise to pay is not secured in any way.[1]

There are other situations in which individuals may want to defer compensation. It is possible for an independent contractor to enter into an arrangement. For example, a director's fee can be deferred through a Deferred Compensation agreement with the employer.[2] No sample of such an agreement is included herein.

Tax Consequences of Deferred Compensation Plans

If a Deferred Compensation agreement is correctly drafted, the employee should incur no current tax liability with regard to the income deferred. Taxation is deferred until the income is received by the employee, the employee's estate, or designated beneficiary. To achieve the desired tax results, the agreement cannot be *formally funded* by giving the employee a nonforfeitable interest in any trust or escrowed fund or in any asset such as a life-insurance policy, annuity, or mutual-fund shares purchased by the employer to informally fund the agreement.

It might, of course, be preferable from the nonowner employee's standpoint if the insurance policy or other funding media could be isolated from the employer's general creditors by placing ownership in an irrevocable trust or escrow account. Such arrangements are known as funded Deferred Compensation plans. Employer contributions to such funded plans will be currently taxable to the employee unless the employee's interest is nontransferable and subject to a substantial risk of forfeiture.[3] In addition, such funded plans may be subject to the participation, vesting, and funding requirements of Title I of ERISA. Since the vesting requirements of ERISA would result in current taxation to the employee, it appears that funded plans will seldom, if ever, be practiced.

An employer may informally fund its Deferred Compensation agreement through the purchase of life-insurance contracts without adverse tax consequences to the employee as long as the funds remain the unrestricted asset of the employer and the employee has no interest in the fund. The IRS has ruled that the employee is not taxable on the premiums paid by the corporation or on any portion of the value of the policy or annuity if the employer applies for, owns, and pays for the policy or annuity contract and uses it merely as a reserve for the employer's obligations under the Deferred Compensation agreement.[4] The employer cannot deduct its premium payments.[5] Any death benefits paid to the employer are free of income tax.[6] An income-tax deduction can be taken by the employer only when payments are actually made to the employee.[7] In order to be deductible, the payments must represent reasonable additional compensation for the employee's services as required by sections 162 and 212 of the code.

At the death of the employee before or after retirement, any payments made to the employee's beneficiary will likely be regarded as "income in respect of a decedent" under IRC Section 691(a).[8] Consequently, such payments will be taxable income to the beneficiary. If the payments to the employee under the agreement are subject to substantial forfeiture provisions both before and after retirement, up to $5,000 of the death benefit is exempt from income tax under IRC Section 101(b).[9] Payments made to the employee will be taxable income when received.

For taxable years beginning after 1976, Deferred Compensation payments to an employee or beneficiary are "personal service income" subject to a maximum income tax rate of 50 percent.[10] Prior to the Tax Reform Act of 1976, Deferred Compensation payments were subject to a maximum tax rate of 70 percent.

The present value of any death benefit payable to the beneficiary will ordinarily be includible in the employee's gross estate for federal estate-tax purposes under IRC Section 2039(a) if at the time before his/her death the employee was receiving, or had an enforceable right to receive at sometime in the future, any lifetime postemployment benefits.[11] However, the beneficiary who receives such payments will be entitled to a tax deduction from gross income for the federal estate tax attributable to the value of the death benefit in the employee's estate.[12]

ERISA Reporting and Disclosure Requirements

Nonqualified Deferred Compensation plans are classified under the Employee Retirement Income Security Act as Employee-Pension-Benefit Plans, which are subject not only to the Title I reporting and disclosure requirement but also to participation, vesting, and funding requirements. However, if a Deferred Compensation plan meets certain requirements it need not meet the participation, vesting, and funding requirements of ERISA, and an *alternative method of compliance* is provided as to reporting and disclosure requirements. The requirements are as follows:

1. The plan must be maintained by an employer primarily for the purpose of providing Deferred Compensation for a select group of management or highly compensated employees.
2. Benefits must be paid solely from the general assets of the employer or be provided exclusively through insurance contracts purchased by the employer from the general assets.

If a Deferred Compensation plan meets these two requirements, all that is required is that the plan administrator file a statement with the Secretary of Labor that includes the employer's name, address, and identification number; a declaration that the employer maintains a plan or plans primarily for the purpose of providing Deferred Compensation for a select group of management or highly compensated employees; and a statement of the number of such plans and the number of employees in each. The statement should be filed within 120 days of the adoption of the plan.

Withholding, Social Security, and Unemployment Taxes

Deferred Compensation payments have been held to be subject to federal income tax withholding.[13] In order for Deferred Compensation payments to an employee not to be classified as wages subject to social security and unemployment taxes, the payments must be due to termination of employment because of death, disability retirement, or retirement after attaining a specified age, and the amounts must be paid under a plan which covers employees generally or a class or classes of employees.[14]

Revenue Ruling 77-25 involved a Deferred Compensation plan established for a company's salaried employees in managerial positions. The company credited amounts to reserve accounts which were to be paid to the executive upon termination of employment at any age for any reason. The company had a separate pension plan which specified that retirement age for its employees was age sixty-five. It was held that payments made by the company to its executives because of and upon or after retirement after attaining age sixty-five were excludible from wages under Section 3121(a)(13) of the Federal Insurance Contributions Act (FICA) and Section 3306(b)(10) of the Federal Unemployment Tax Act (FUTA).

In Revenue Ruling 78-263 the circumstances were sufficiently different to result in a ruling that the payments were *wages* for Social Security and unemployment tax purposes. A company established a Deferred Compensation plan for its officers under which they were to receive monthly payments for seven years commencing the first day of the month following retirement. The plan did not specify a retirement age. The company had a qualified pension plan under which officers could retire at age sixty-five. An officer of the company retired at age sixty and began receiving payments under the Deferred Compensation plan. Since the employee in this case was not eligible for retirement under the company's pension plan until age sixty-five, the payments under the Deferred Compensation plan were held to be *wages* subject to FICA and FUTA tax.

Normally, the IRS has primary responsibility for interpreting the Federal Insurance Contributions Act. However, where wages are from employment which is not covered by FICA and employer contributions are required, as in the case of state employees, the Social Security Administration determines whether and when employer contributions are due. The definition of wages is the same in the Social Security Act and in FICA. There have been two Social Security Administration rulings as to whether postretirement Deferred Compensation payments were *wages*. SSR 73-30 held that payments were subject to tax in a situation where an employment contract provided for retirement benefits of $15,000 annually. It was held that the payments arose from previously earned but deferred wages and were not wages due to retirement. In a later ruling, SSR 75-2, it was held that the payments were not *wages* in a situation where state employees entered into Deferred Compensation agreements with their employer. The difference between the two rulings was that in SSR 73-30 the deferral was not voluntary because it was part of the employment agreement. In SSR 75-2, the employees had a choice of either currently receiving wages or electing to defer them. SSR 75-2 holds that when the deferral is *voluntary* the amounts deferred will be *wages* when deferred, not when payments are received after retirement. This is preferable, since the employee will usually already be paying the maximum Social-Security tax and no additional tax will be due during the employee's working years.

In summary, it appears that in order to have Deferred Compensation payments following retirement constitute *wages* for Social-Security purposes when the income is deferred, rather than when payments are made by the employer, it is advisable for the employer to establish a plan for a class or classes of employees, such as officers or managerial employees, by adopting a resolution. Individual agreements should then be entered into which specify retirement age when payments are to begin. The Deferred Compensation agreements should not be part of an employment contract. If the agreement provides for nonforfeitable benefits in the event of voluntary termination of employment before retirement, payments commencing upon termination of employment will no doubt constitute wages upon which the employer must make Social-Security contributions. The sample resolutions and agreements which follow have been drafted with these considerations in mind.

The Social Security Administration has ruled in SSR 73-30 that Deferred Compensation payments (even if subject to social security tax) represent amounts *earned* previously in the performance of past services. As such, they do not reduce the employee's Social Security benefits.

Notes

1. Rev. Rul. 60-31, Rev. Rul. 70-435, *Comm. v. Oates,* 207 F.2d 711 acq.; *Comm. v. Olmsted Inc. Life Agency,* 304 F.2d 16; *Ray S. Robinson,* 44 TC 20, acq.; *Howard Veit,* 8 TC 809, acq.; *Basil F. Basila,* 36 TC 111, acq.; *Ernest K. Gann,* 31 TC 211, acq.

2. Rev. Rul. 71-419.

3. Prop. Treas. Reg. Sec., 1.402(b)-1(a)(2).

4. Rev. Rul. 68-99; Rev. Rul. 72-25.

5. IRC Sec. 264(a)(1).

6. IRC Sec. 101(a)(1).

7. IRC Sec. 404(a)(5); *Trinity Construction Co. Inc.* (CA-5, 1970); *Lundy Packing Company v. U.S.,* 302 F. Supp. 182.

8. Estate of Irving S. Wright, 336 F.2d 121, aff'g 39 TC 597; *Essenfeld v. Comm.* 311 F.2d 208; *Estate of Edward Bausch,* 186 F.2d 313 aff'g 14 TC 1433; *Estate of Edgar B. O'Daniel*, 173 F.2d 966.

9. Rev. Rul. 71-361; Rev. Rul. 73-327.

10. IRC Sec. 1348(b).

11. *All v. McCobb,* 321 F.2d 633; *Bahen's Est. v. U.S.,* 305 F.2d 827; *Estate of Edward H. Wadewitz,* 339 F.2d 980.

12. IRC Sec. 691(c)(1)(A).

13. IRC Sec. 3401(a); Rev. Rul. 69-286; Rev. Rul. 77-25.

14. IRC Sec. 3121(a)(13); Rev. Rul. 69-286; Rev. Rul. 71-456; Rev. Rul. 77-25.

Appendix D
Sample Resolution Establishing a Deferred Compensation Plan for a Class of Employees

The following sample resolution establishes a Deferred Compensation plan for key managerial employees of the corporation. As stated in the forword for counsel, Revenue Ruling 77-25 held that payments from a plan, established by the employer that makes provision for a class of employees, are not subject to Social Security taxes if the payments are made after retirement at an age either specified in the plan or in a separate pension plan. That is, the payments will not constitute "wages" for Social Security purposes.

I, _____, Secretary of _____, a corporation duly organized and existing under and by virtue of the laws of the State of _____, DO HEREBY CERTIFY;

That on the _____ day of _____, 19____, a meeting of the Directors of said corporation was duly called and held at _____, at which a quorum was present, and the following resolution was unanimously adopted by said Board of Directors, to wit:

WHEREAS, the corporation, as an inducement and motivation to its key managerial employees, desires to create a Deferred Compensation Plan;

THEREFORE, BE IT RESOLVED, that this corporation hereby establishes a Deferred Compensation Plan in accordance with the following:

Purpose. The purpose of the Deferred Compensation Plan, hereafter called the "Plan", is to provide benefits for the corporation's eligible employees at death, disability or retirement at or after attainment of age 65.

Eligibility. The Plan shall be for the benefit of key managerial employees of this corporation as determined by its Board of Directors.

Agreement. The Corporation shall enter into a Deferred Compensation Agreement with each eligible employee. Such Agreement shall be substantially identical to the blank "Deferred Compensation Agreement" attached hereto.

Amendment and Termination. The Plan shall be subject to amendment or termination at any time by the Board of Directors; provided, however, that such amendment or termination shall not affect any Deferred Compensation Agreement entered into prior to such amendment or termination.

IN WITNESS WHEREOF, I have hereunto set my hand and the seal of the Corporation in the city of _____, State of _____, on the _____ day of _____, 19____.

Appendix E
Sample Deferred Compensation Agreement with Employee

This Agreement entered into this _____ day of _____ 19___, by and between _____, a domestic corporation having its principal office in _____, hereafter called the "Corporation," and _____, a resident of _____County, _____, hereafter called the "Employee,"

WITNESSETH:

WHEREAS, the Employee has been employed by the Corporation for _____ years and is now employed by the Corporation in the capacity of _____;

WHEREAS, the Corporation desires to retain the services of the Employee in an executive capacity and is aware that it would suffer financial loss should the Employee enter the employment of a competitor; and

Whereas, the Employee is willing to continue his/her employment provided the Corporation will agree to make certain payments following said Employee's retirement (death) (or) (disability).

NOW THEREFORE, in consideration of the services heretofore rendered and to be rendered by the Employee and the mutual covenants contained herein, the parties agree as follows:

1. RETIREMENT INCOME. If the Employee remains continuously employed by the Corporation on a full-time basis until his/her retirement from active employment on or after the first day of the month next following his/her sixty-fifth birthday, then beginning in the month of such retirement, the Corporation will pay to the Employee monthly installments of $ _____ (amount may also be written out) for _____ months. If the Employee dies after retirement but prior to receiving _____ monthly installments of Deferred Compensation as herein provided, the remaining monthly installments of Deferred Compensation shall be paid to the Employee's "Beneficiary" as defined in Article (2)(3) hereof.

   OPTIONAL ARTICLE PROVIDING PRE-RETIREMENT
   DEATH BENEFIT

2. PRE-RETIREMENT DEATH BENEFIT. If the Employee dies prior to retirement and while in full-time employment with the Corporation, the Corporation shall, beginning in the month following the Employee's death, pay monthly installments of $_____ (amount may also be written out) for _____ to the employee's "Beneficiary" as defined in Article 3 hereof.

Many Deferred Compensation plans which are informally funded with life insurance provide for preretirement death benefits. The monthly installments will usually be the same as the retirement benefit. The installments may be less, however, if the employer wishes to retain some of the death benefit for key-employee indemnification.

---

3. BENEFICIARY. In the event of the Employee's death, any remaining installments provided for in Article 1 hereof (or any monthly installments becom_____ hereof) shall be paid to (the AB_____, Anystate, as Trustee under a _____ _____) (the Employee's Sp_____ving, otherwise to _____). (NOTE TO ATTORNEY: Choose only one of the above options.) The Beneficiary named herein may be changed at any _____ by the Employee, with the agreement of the Corporation, by wr_____.

If upon the death of the Employee there is no trust in existence qualified to receive _____ payment (neither _____ _____ survi_____, or upon the death of the last survivor of them if either of them survives the employee). (NOTE TO ATTORNEY: Again, choose one of the listed options.) The commuted value of any amounts remaining unpaid shall be paid in one sum to the executor or administrator of the estate of (the Employee) (the last survivor of the Employee or his/her designated beneficiaries.) The commuted value referred to in this agreement shall be the total sum of such payments discounted at the rate of _____% per annum, compounded annually.

From an estate-planning standpoint, maximum income- and estate-tax advantages often may be achieved by designating the trustee of an inter vivos trust as beneficiary of any death benefits. Discretionary dispositive provisions in the trust may enable the trustee to divide the income among several tax entities or direct it to beneficiaries in lower tax brackets.

OPTIONAL ARTICLE PROVIDING DISABILITY BENEFITS

4. DISABILITY BENEFITS. In the event the Employee becomes totally disabled prior to age 65, the Corporation shall make (monthly /annual) payments of $_____ to the Employee. Such payments shall be in lieu of salary and shall begin six months after the commencement of such disability and shall continue until whichever of the following events first occurs:

    A. benefits become payable under some other provision of this Agreement,

    B. such disability ceases, or

    C. the obligation of the Corporation under this Agreement terminate for any of the reasons provided.

As used in this Agreement, the term "totally disabled" means disability which completely prevents the Employee from working for pay or profit in any occupation for which the Employee is reasonably fitted by education, training or experience; provided, however, that the Employee shall not be considered totally disabled if the total disability resulted from an intentional self-injury or from injury occurring or disease contracted before this Agreement takes effect.

OPTIONAL ARTICLE PROVIDING FORFEITURE PROVISIONS

5. FORFEITURE PROVISIONS. The Employee shall forfeit all rights in and to any benefits payable under the terms of this Agreement if:

A. The Employee dies by suicide within two years from the date of this Agreement.

B. The Employee voluntarily leaves the Corporation's service before his/her attainment of age sixty-five (65).

C. He/She is discharged for any cause prior to the Employee's attainment of age sixty-five (65).

D. The Employee is discharged for proper cause after his/her attainment of age sixty-five (65). The term "proper cause" shall include, but shall not be limited to:

    (1) failure to perform assigned duties with reasonable skill and diligence,

    (2) gross misconduct, or

    (3) conviction of a felony.

E. The Employee competes with the Corporation in violation of Article 7 and 9 hereof.

F. He/She fails to perform advisory services as required by Article 8 and 9 hereof.

The employee's right to receive future payments need not be forfeitable or contingent in order to avoid current taxation. However, it may be advisable to include one or more of the above conditions for business reasons. Care should be exercised in coordinating the suicide clause with the provisions of any insurance policy purchased by the employer to informally fund the agreement. It may be advisable to provide for forfeiture in the event of suicide even if no other forfeiture provisions are included to avoid any possibility of a substantial corporate liability which is not covered by the receipt of death benefits due to an exclusion clause in the insurance policy.

VESTING

6. VESTING. If the Employee voluntarily or involuntarily terminates full-time employment with the corporation for reasons other than death, disability or retirement prior to the first day of the month next following the Employee's sixty-fifth birthday, and at the time of such termination His/Her full years of service with the corporation added to His/Her age is greater than seventy, the benefits under this Agreement shall be fully vested.

A wide choice of formulae can be employed in vesting. A proportional reduction in benefits for premature termination is often wise and the agreement not to compete may, for business reasons, be advisable. If the agreement is employee motivated and the employee has entered into the agreement in lieu of a salary increase, immediate progressive vesting may be necessary. It is usual to prohibit anticipation of benefits prior to normal retirement to avoid creating a competitor. Premature termination for reduced benefits is often funded by using the option to obtain a paid-up policy in a reduced amount. The tax savings to the corporation and the time value of money in making installment payments can be taken into consideration.

OPTIONAL COVENANT NOT TO COMPETE

7. AGREEMENT NOT TO COMPETE. The Employee agrees that after said Employee's retirement, and/or so long as he/she continues to receive monthly payments hereunder, the Employee will not directly or indirectly enter into or in any manner take part in, any business, profession or other endeavor, either as an employee, agent, independent contractor, owner or otherwise, in the city of _____ which, in the opinion of the Board of Directors of the Corporation, shall be in competition with the business of the Corporation, and in this connection the opinion of the Board of Directors shall be final and conclusive.

OPTIONAL COVENANT TO PROVIDE ADVISORY SERVICES

8. ADVISORY SERVICES. The Employee agrees that as long as said Employee continues to receive monthly installments hereunder and as long as he/she is physically and mentally able to do so, the Employee will render the Employer, as an independent contractor, such advise, counsel or other services as the Employer may reasonably and from time to time require but not such as would constitute full-time rendering of services. For such advice, counsel and other services as the Employee may render in accordance with the provisions of this Article, he/she shall be compensated by the Employer, as an independent contractor, at the same rate as his/her cash compensation rate immediately prior to retirement. In addition, the Employer shall reimburse the Employee for reasonable travel expense from whatever place the Employee may then be living and for other reasonable expenses incurred by said Employee in rendering such advisory services.

9. OPTIONAL BREACH OF COVENANTS ARTICLE. The Employee agrees that if he/she shall breach any covenant of Article 7 herein not to compete (or of Article 8 herein to provide advisory services) and shall continue to breach such covenant for a period of thirty (30) days after the Corporation shall have requested said Employee to desist from such breach, then, any provisions hereof to the contrary notwithstanding, no further payments shall be due or payable by the Corporation hereunder either to the Employee or to the Beneficiary designated in Article (2) (3) hereof.

10. OTHER BENEFITS. Nothing contained herein shall in any way limit the Employee's right to participate in or benefit from any pension, profit-sharing or other retirement plan for which said Employee is or may become eligible by reason of his/her employment. Nor shall this Agreement replace any contract of employment, whether oral or written, between the Corporation and the Employee but shall be considered a supplement thereto.

11. NON SECURED PROMISE. The rights of the Employee under this Agreement and of any beneficiary of the Employee shall be solely those of an unsecured creditor of the Corporation. Any insurance policy or any other asset acquired or held by the Corporation in connection with the liabilities assumed by it hereunder, shall not, except as otherwise expressly provided, be deemed to be held under any trust for the benefit of the Employee or his beneficiaries or to be security for the performance of the obligations of the Corporation, but shall be, and remain, a general unpledged, unrestricted asset of the Corporation.

12. CHANGE OF BUSINESS FORM. The Corporation agrees that it will not merge or consolidate with any other corporation or organization, or permit its business activities to be taken over by any other organization, unless and until the succeeding or continuing corporation or other organization shall expressly assume the rights and obligations of the Corporation herein set forth. The Corporation further agrees that it will not cease its business activities or terminate its existence, other than as heretofore set forth in this Paragraph 12, without having made adequate provision for the fulfilling of its obligations hereunder. In the event of any default with respect to the provisions of this Paragraph 12, the Employee (or other obligee or obligees) shall have a continuing lien on all corporate assets, including already transferred assets, until such default be corrected.

13. LEAVE OF ABSENCE. The Corporation may, in its sole discretion, permit the Employee to take a leave of absence for a period not to exceed one year. During this time the Employee will be considered to be still in the employ of the Corporation for purposes of this Agreement.

14. WITHHOLDING. Notwithstanding any of the foregoing provisions hereof, the Corporation may withhold from any payment to be made hereunder such amounts as it may be required to withhold under any applicable federal, state or other law, and transmit such withheld amounts to the applicable taxing authority.

15. GOVERNING LAW. This Agreement shall be governed and construed in accordance with the laws of the State of _____.

16. JOINDER OF SPOUSE. The Spouse of the Employee hereby joins in this Agreement to acknowledge his/her consent to the terms of this Agreement.

This provision for joinder of spouse usually will be included if the state whose law governs is a community property state.

17. COUNTERPARTS. This Agreement may be executed in an original and any number of counterparts, each of which shall constitute an original of one and the same instrument.

18. AMENDMENT. During the lifetime of the Employee, this Agreement may be amended or revoked at any time in whole or in part by the mutual written agreement of the Parties.

IN WITNESS WHEREOF, the parties hereto have set their names, the Corporation by its duly authorized officer, the day and year first above written.

THE XYZ CORPORATION

BY _____

ATTEST: _____

_____   _____

Appendix F
Sample Resolution
Authorizing Funding

I, _____, Secretary of _____, a corporation duly organized and existing under and by virtue of the laws of the State of _____ DO HEREBY CERTIFY:

That on the _____ day of _____, 19____, a meeting of the Board of Directors of said Corporation was duly called and held at _____, at which a quorum was present and the following resolutions were unanimously adopted by said Board of Directors, to wit:

WHEREAS, _____ is currently employed by the corporation in the capacity of _____;

WHEREAS, the Corporation and _____ entered into an agreement on the _____ day of _____, 19____, providing for the payment by the Corporation of certain amounts in the nature of Deferred Compensation of the services of said Employee which amounts are to be paid following said Employee's (retirement), (disability), or (death); and

WHEREAS, it is felt that an insurance policy on the life of _____, purchased by the Corporation, would best protect and compensate the Corporation for any financial loss resulting from said Employee's death and would provide the Corporation with readily available funds with which to meet part or all of its obligations under the Deferred Compensation Agreement described above;

THEREFORE, BE IT RESOLVED, that the Deferred Compensation agreement entered into by and between _____ and _____ on the _____ day of _____, 19____, is hereby approved and ratified and said Agreement shall be effective as of the date of its execution; and

(BE IT FURTHER RESOLVED, that the Corporation does hereby approve and ratify the purchase of a _____ policy (with Waiver of Premium Disability Benefit) from _____ Company upon the life of _____ in the amount of $_____ with the Corporation designated as owner and beneficiary; and)

(BE IT FURTHER RESOLVED, that the Corporation shall maintain the above policy in full force and effect and shall pay all premiums when due; all rights and benefits accruing from said policy shall belong solely to the Corporation, and _____ shall have no interest whatsoever in the insurance contract; the cash value of said policy, if any, shall be carried on the books of the Corporation as an unassigned asset and the Board of Directors shall have the right to assign, encumber, sell or dispose of said policy in any manner it may please and to receive any value of the policy for the benefit of the Corporation.)

The wording used herein should coincide with the provisions of the Deferred Compensation agreement.

IN WITNESS WHEREOF, I have hereunto set my hand and the seal of the corporation in the city of _____, State of _____, on the _____ day of _____, 19____.

_____

The corporation's counsel might prefer to separate the insurance provisions and the ratification of the Deferred Compensation agreement into two resolutions. In any event, it is recommended that the two items of business be handled as separate provisions.

Appendix G
Defense Acquisition
Regulations

Deferred Compensation plans are an allowable expense insofar as they do not constitute unreasonable compensation to the employee and are for services rendered during the contract period. There is, however, a particular sensitivity to plans in which the participants are the principals of the firm where it needs to be established that the plan is not simply a funnel for profits and/or avoidance of paying out corporate dividends. Armed Services Procurement Regulations 15-205.6 specifically refers to Deferred Compensation in treating what is reasonable compensation for personal services:

> (1) (CWAS) Compensation for personal services includes all remuneration paid currently or accrued, in whatever form and whether paid immediately or deferred, for services rendered by employees to the contractor during the period of contract performance . . .[1]

The Deferred Compensation referred to is the more generic definition, that is, including pensions, profit sharing, and other forms beyond the definition as used in this text. The regulations go on to define Deferred Compensation in the same section under (f):

> (1) As used herein, Deferred Compensation includes all remuneration, in whatever form, for which the employee is not paid until the lapse of a stated period of years or the occurrence of other events as provided in the plans except that it does not include normal end of accounting period accruals. It includes (i) contributions to pension (including early retirement), annuity, stock bonus, and profit sharing plans, (ii) contributions to disability, withdrawal, insurance, survivorship, and similar benefit plans, and (iii) other Deferred Compensation whether paid in cash or in stock.[2]

The costs would automatically become allowable for qualified plans if they meet the test of the IRS for tax deductibility during the current period, but the regulations also provide for legitimately incurred costs that are not tax deductible as well: Deferred Compensation, as used in this text, " . . . is not subject to the limitations of the Internal Revenue Code and the regulations thereunder."[3]

The allowability seems to be straightforward where the incurred liability is equal to life-insurance premiums paid and under (v) even as it may apply to owners:

15-205.16(a)(1) Costs of insurance required or approved, and maintained pursuant to the contract, are allowable.[4]

(2) Costs of other insurance maintained by the contractor in connection with the general conduct of his business are allowable . . . [5]

(v) Costs of insurance on the lives of officers, partners or proprietors are allowable only to the extent that insurance represents additional compensations.[6]

If the contractor were to take the position that something greater than the premium outlay would be the allocatable current expense for the plan, this would seem to call for the concurrence of the contract monitor. The difference might be regarded as self-insurance, and provisions are made in the regulations for self-insurance. They do require approval and "if purchased insurance is available, the charge for any self-insurance . . . shall not exceed the cost of comparable purchased insurance . . . "[7] 15-205.16(4)(b). This seems to suggest that the rather larger cost of what in this text has been described as the traditional method might be considered allowable.

Another area to which the contractor should be alert is that of contingencies. If the plan is drawn in such a way that a participant has a substantial likelihood of becoming disenfranchised, the current period allocation of cost may be unallowable. The regulations do not preclude funding for contingencies as such, but recognize that they could be an unwarranted drain-off of expense if the contingencies never ripen into obligations. The plan can, of course, be designed to vest in such a way that the contingency element is removed. Again concurrence of the contract monitor seems to be advisable if the benefits are to any degree contingent.

Notes

1. Department of Defense, Armed Services Procurement Regulations, 15-205.6 (Washington, D.C.: U.S. Government Printing Office.
    2. Ibid., 15-205.6(f).
    3. Ibid., 15-205.6(f)(2)(ii).
    4. Ibid., 15-205.16(a)(1).
    5. Ibid.
    6. Ibid.
    7. Ibid., 15-205.16(4)(b).

Appendix H
Table of Net
Present Value

Net Present Value Calculation

Compute the net present value of a payment of $12,000 per year each year for thirteen years paid at the end of the year at 12 percent interest:

$$6.424 \times \$12,000 = \$77,088$$

At 20 percent interest

$$4.533 \times \$12,000 = \$54,396$$

Note: If the payments were $1,000 per month paid at the end of each month for 156 months (thirteen years) the net present value at 12 percent would be $78,822.94 and at 20 percent it would be $55,447.06. This calculation can not be made from the table and is simply illustrative of the difference of which the plan designer should be cognizant.

The three place table is accurate to $10-$20 in the range of sums usually used in Deferred Compensation.

Net Present Value of Payments of One Dollar per Year Paid at the End of Each Year

	Percentage							
	8	10	12	14	16	18	20	22
1	.926	.909	.893	.877	.0862	.847	.833	.820
2	1.783	1.736	1.690	1.647	1.605	1.566	1.528	1.492
3	2.577	2.487	2.402	2.322	2.246	2.174	2.106	2.042
4	3.312	3.170	3.037	2.914	2.798	2.690	2.589	2.494
5	3.993	3.791	3.605	3.433	3.274	3.127	2.991	2.864
6	4.623	4.355	4.111	3.889	3.685	3.498	3.326	3.167
7	5.206	4.668	4.564	4.288	4.039	3.811	3.605	3.416
8	5.747	5.335	4.968	4.639	4.344	4.078	3.837	3.619
9	6.247	5.759	5.328	4.946	4.607	4.303	4.031	3.786
10	6.710	6.145	5.690	5.216	4.833	4.494	4.192	3.923
11	7.139	6.495	5.938	5.453	5.029	4.656	4.327	4.035
12	7.536	6.817	6.194	5.660	5.197	4.793	4.439	4.127
13	7.904	7.103	6.424	5.842	5.342	4.910	4.533	4.203
14	8.244	7.367	6.628	6.002	5.468	5.008	4.611	4.265
15	8.559	7.606	6.811	6.142	5.575	5.092	4.675	4.315
16	8.851	7.824	6.974	6.265	5.668	5.162	4.730	4.357
17	9.122	8.023	7.120	6.373	5.749	5.222	4.775	4.391
18	9.372	8.201	7.250	6.467	5.918	5.273	4.812	4.419
19	9.604	8.364	7.366	6.550	5.877	5.316	4.843	4.442
20	9.818	8.514	7.470	6.623	5.929	5.353	4.870	4.460
21	10.017	8.649	7.562	6.687	5.973	5.383	4.890	4.476
22	10.201	8.772	7.645	6.743	6.011	5.410	4.920	4.488
23	10.371	8.832	7.718	6.792	6.044	5.432	4.925	4.500
24	10.529	8.985	7.784	6.835	6.073	5.451	4.937	4.507
25	10.675	9.077	7.843	6.873	6.097	5.467	4.948	4.514

Appendix I
Outline of Benefits

Benefits to Employee

A lifetime income starting at age _____ of $_____ year.

A minimum payment after retirement starts of $_____ (for an early death after retirement).

An income to spouse (or nominee) of $_____ per year for _____ years if participant dies anytime prior to retirement.

A disability income if disabled prior to age sixty equal to the annual cost of funding, plus full benefit at retirement or due to premature death.

No income tax on funds being accumulated during working life (tax deferred to lower tax period).

$5,000 deduction for first payment to spouse after death.

No P.S. 58 or Table I tax on the economic benefit (as on group-life insurance in excess of $50,000).

Escape agreement if the firm's accumulation is jeopardized by claims of other creditors.

Vesting or contractual ownership.

Exclusion from Social Security deductions for the deferred amount.

Benefits to Employer

Tax deductibility of all benefit payments to employee when paid.

Tax deductibility of all payments to spouse in case of premature death.

Funds flow at death of employee—a tax free addition to surplus: discounted to present value versus obligation; key person indemnification available.

Option to continue mortality after retirement.

Freedom from tax on excess accumulation of profits.

Little or no balance sheet or income-statement impact (ownership of funding by employer).

Freedom of choice as to employees, amounts, retirement dates.

Stop/start funding without permission or penalty.

Absence of obligations for qualification or periodic filing IRS/ERISA.

No Social Security contribution (if applicable).

Index

Accelerated vanishing premium, 44
Accrual of liability, 66
Agreements, 101
Annuity, 12, 31, 60, 82, 83
Annuity, life and certain, 83
Annuity due, 22
Authorization, 117

Balance sheet, 65
Bookkeeping entries, 68
Bond of benefits, 1, 25

Cash flow, 72
Constructive receipt, 76
Contingency reserve, 19
Covenant not to compete, 114
Cross-pooling, 80
CSO Table, 95, 96
Current assumption life, 83

Defense Acquisition Regulation, 119
Deferred Compensation defined, xv, 1
Defined benefit, 3
Defined contribution, 2
Disability, 20
Discriminatory advantage, 1, 87

Entity concept, 66
ERISA, reporting and disclosure, 78, 105
Escrow accounts, 76
Excess-profits tax, 4, 7, 67

FICA, 106
401(k), 3
Fund flow leverage, 21
Funding media, 14, 43
Funding targets, 26
FUTA, 106

Golden handcuffs, 1, 25
Group pensions, 2

Income statement, 65
Internalized funds, 6
Investments, 6
IRA, 2

Journal entries, 69

Keogh, 2

Legal comments, 103
Leverage of mortality, 19
Life income, 12
Life premium to sixty-five, 44
Life premium to seventy, 44
Life premium to ninety-five, 14, 43

Maslow's hierarchy of needs, 86
Minimum deposit, 60, 72, 77
Mortality funding, 19
Mortality tables, 96
Motivation, 86

Need for change, 9
Need for review, 22
Net present value, 31, 121
Non-compete clause, 26, 27, 114

Ordinary life, 43
Outline of benefits, 123
Overfunding, 11

Pre-retirement death, 111
Probability, 17, 34
Provisional participants, 20

Qualified Plans, 2, 3, 5

Resolutions, 103, 109
Retired lives reserve, 6
Reverse discrimination, 4
Risk transfer, 23

Safety net, 14, 19, 43
Security for firm, 5
Side funds, 83
Sinking fund, 82, 83
Social Security, 5, 7, 8
Split dollar, 77
Start-Stop, 15, 72, 77
Substandard mortality, 98
Suicide, 113
Survival of the firm, 5, 21

About the Authors

Robert J. Hansman is president of Hansman McAvoy & Co., Inc., a risk-management and insurance-brokerage firm located in Hingham, Massachusetts. A graduate of Harvard University, he is a practitioner who has long advocated the use of proven risk-management techniques in financial planning. Mr. Hansman is chairman of the Insurance Benefits Committee of the Professional Insurance Agents National Association, the author of a number of articles and books, and a frequent lecturer on life, property and casualty insurance, risk management, and financial planning. Mr. Hansman is a member of the American Society of Chartered Life Underwriters.

John W. Larrabee is vice-president of financial services with Hansman McAvoy & Co., Inc., and is a graduate of Harvard University. Specializing in the design and marketing of Deferred Compensation plans, Mr. Larrabee is a frequent lecturer on life insurance and is coauthor with Mr. Hansman of an article on funding Deferred Compensation with mortality. Mr. Larrabee is a member of the American Society of Chartered Life Underwriters.